the less is more garden

the less is more garden

BIG IDEAS FOR DESIGNING YOUR SMALL YARD

susan morrison

Timber Press
Portland, Oregon

Frontispiece: Small spaces can help us appreciate gardening's simple pleasures.

Photography and design credits appear on page 215.

Published in 2018 by Timber Press, Inc.
The Haseltine Building
133 S.W. Second Avenue, Suite 450
Portland, Oregon 97204-3527
timberpress.com

Printed in China

Book design by Debbie Berne Design

ISBN: 978-1-60469-791-9

Library of Congress Cataloging-in-Publication Data

Names: Morrison, Susan, 1963– author.
Title: The less is more garden: big ideas for designing your small
  yard / Susan Morrison
Description: Portland, Oregon: Timber Press, 2018. | Includes
  bibliographical references and index.
Identifiers: LCCN 2017046011 (print) | LCCN 2017049480
  (ebook) | ISBN 9781604698398 | ISBN 9781604697919 (hardcover)
Subjects: LCSH: Gardens–Design.
Classification: LCC SB473 (ebook) | LCC SB473 .M68 2018 (print) | DDC
  712–dc23
LC record available at https://lccn.loc.gov/2017046011

To my mother, Pat Morrison, for being my gardening inspiration, and to my sister Kathy Hawes, who may not know the difference between a daylily and a daphne, but is always my biggest cheerleader.

contents

foreword

Every time I visit a well-designed small garden it makes me feel envious. These spaces, which are a quarter – or less – the size of my one-acre property, have more interest, impact, charm, and style than I can imagine for my landscape. As the editor of a national gardening magazine, it is my job to find these spaces that inspire the rest of us to try to improve our own gardens. What the best of these gardens have in common is understanding one simple concept: less is more.

When confronted with something that isn't turning out the way we'd hoped, be it a recipe, a living room design, or a garden, our impulse is to add something. That thing we add might just be the key to success. When it is not, we add something else. And things still aren't working. What we wind up with is something so full of competing flavors, color, tchotchkes, or plants that we can't even tell what the problem is anymore. Small spaces offer little room for error, so the stakes are higher.

Fortunately, you have this book. Many books on small-space garden design are filled with random, trendy ideas the author merely imagined or happened to have a photo of. This one, however, is written by a real, down-in-the-trenches designer who is as concerned with practicality as she is with beauty. Susan has designed countless small spaces, successful in no small part because she listens intently to the cares and concerns of her clients. This grasp of the hopes, fears, desires, and struggles of people who want the most from their limited space makes her uniquely qualified to help you handle yours.

If you listen to what Susan is saying in this book, and internalize the principles she is proposing, I have little doubt that the garden you create will make me feel envious, too.

— Steve Aitken, editor, *Fine Gardening* magazine

A small deck surrounded by a small garden makes a perfect spot for relaxing.

preface

the less is more approach to garden design

Once upon a time, small gardens were mainly confined to the condos, courtyards, and terraces of crowded urban areas. In contrast, the typical suburban landscape tended to be large and sprawling. But in the past forty years, America's suburban lots have shrunk, from the Southeast to the Midwest to the West Coast. In fact, the term small garden is gradually losing its meaning, as many of us live on a quarter, an eighth, or even less of an acre. Urban and suburban aren't so different anymore. Small has become the new normal.

In my practice as a landscape designer, most of the backyards I design measure less than 2500 square feet; layouts are rarely more than 40 by 60 feet. I no longer think of that as small; it has become standard. Interestingly, while active gardeners are often concerned with fitting everything into a space that is generally smaller than the backyards they grew up in, I am just as likely to hear from homeowners more interested in creating a space that will be as simple as possible to maintain. In our time-crunched, overworked, two-career society, taking the time to envision, create, and maintain a garden can seem overwhelming. No one wants another to-do list item, but most of us want a backyard that's a refuge: a place where we can unwind, entertain, and enjoy ourselves in whatever forms those pursuits take.

This shift in how we live, work, and play is what led me to develop the less is more approach to garden design and outdoor living. My clients want to spend more time enjoying the outdoors, but less time fussing with and maintaining their space. I understand what they're looking for, because the hypothetical family I've described could be mine.

I spent my middle school and teenage years in a ranch-style home on a quarter-acre lot in Southern California. While the house was a mere 1600 square feet, the large backyard more than made up for the elbow bumping my family of four tolerated inside. We spent as much time as we could outdoors. Our backyard was home to a swimming pool, two full-sized patios, flower beds, fruit trees, and a vegetable garden, not to mention plenty of lawn on which to play games and run around. With that much space, it's easy to accommodate an active, multi-generational, outdoor lifestyle. Of course, my childhood memories aren't just about fun in the sun. Looking after a space that big took a lot of effort. Growing up as the designated lawn mower and pool cleaner meant my Saturday mornings weren't exactly my own.

Fast-forward to my first house in a newly constructed development. Despite the fact that the backyard was a fraction of the size of my childhood home's yard, I did what so many of us do, and modeled the landscape on what I had growing up. While I didn't have the space or the budget for a swimming pool, I replicated the garden I remembered as closely as I could. I made sure there was lots of lawn, and surrounded it with beautiful flower beds. This only left room for one smallish patio, and no dedicated areas to grow a few tomato plants, or to enjoy a good book or a nap. As for practical considerations, such as privacy screening from my all-too-close neighbors, well, I didn't think about that until *after* I'd filled all my planting beds with blooming shrubs and annuals.

While we enjoyed our sunny backyard, my husband and I spent far less time outside than my family had while I was growing up. And because I had created a landscape that included two of the most time-intensive aspects of garden care – a lawn and fussy flowers – the small space required a lot of effort to maintain. This became a problem for two busy professionals who traveled a lot, as yard upkeep was constantly at the top of our chore list. (More so for my husband than for me. After all those years chained to a weekly mowing schedule, I refused to ever push a lawnmower again.)

We eventually moved to a new home in Northern California, where we finally got it right. Our new backyard was even smaller – only 18 feet deep by 60 feet wide. But this time, I embraced the less is more philosophy. At its heart, this approach to garden design means:

- Less space, more enjoyment
- Less effort, more beauty
- Less maintenance, more relaxation
- Less gardening-by-the-numbers, more YOU

The pleasure I took in creating the garden of my dreams is what inspired me to trade in my business suits and briefcase for jeans and a drafting table. As a garden designer, I discovered many of my clients were making the same mistakes I had with my first garden. Despite living in California, my typical clients are not movie stars or dot-com millionaires. They are ordinary people just like me, looking to get the most out of modest-sized lots, while juggling jobs, kids, and busy lives.

If this describes you, and you are hoping to get more out of your garden with less time and effort, this book will help you. Twelve years of designing gardens and consulting with homeowners has taught me that the same issues come up over and over again, regardless of budget or lifestyle goals. Whether you are designing a new landscape from the ground up, rehabilitating an existing one, or just hoping to take your current yard to a new level with a few easy fixes, the less is more approach to garden design will get you there.

the lifestyle garden

It doesn't take long for a garden designer to learn that designing for real clients is very different than designing on paper. A lovingly rendered backyard plan may successfully incorporate classic design principles like rhythm, unity, and scale – and be a beautiful piece of artwork – but if it will never exist in the real world, it doesn't need to be practical. Conversely, many homeowners skip straight to the practical, beginning design consultations with a laundry list of garden elements to include and problem areas to address. But without laying a foundation based on lifestyle goals, there is a significant risk the design won't be an accurate reflection of what the homeowner hopes to achieve. This foundation is even more important when the space involved is that of today's typical home, which is far from expansive. A better approach is to set design objectives not based on decks or structures or even plants, but rather on how the space will be used.

Part of planning a new garden includes considering how it will be used.

To help clients figure this out, I've developed key questions based on the three Ws. These aren't traditional design considerations, but I have found them invaluable.

- What will you be doing in the garden?
- When will you be outside?
- Who will be with you?

Beginning with the three Ws often leads to a completely different design than what homeowners initially envision. For example, I once consulted with a couple who had three small children. The family spent a lot of time outside, and wanted their backyard to be more attractive, as well as more practical. This was a newer home, and the backyard was organized in the typical style of what I like to call "the contractor's special"—a concrete rectangular patio leading to a rectangular lawn, with a thin moustache of plants around the edge.

Families often need a garden design that can evolve with kids' changing activities.

right A curving path winds through the garden, creating a track for kids' games as well as for adults to admire the greenery.

Defining their goals was easy. They wanted to maintain play space and make the backyard look bigger. Most homeowners would assume, as they did, that the solution would be to increase the size of the lawn at the expense of the already-small planting beds. In design-speak, I could have said that making the largest element in their backyard even larger would throw off the scale and balance even more than it was currently, but how meaningful would that have been? Instead, I focused on creating a design that addressed their lifestyle goals: family time in a beautiful but modest outdoor space.

One of the first things I noticed was the crowded patio, stuffed to overflowing with furniture and kids' playthings. No point in suggesting they try to declutter; the "stuff" was an inevitable byproduct of their active, outdoor lifestyle. Instead, our solution was to expand the size of the patio. This initially felt counter-intuitive to them because it meant devoting less space to greenery. But because it was the first thing visible when one entered the space, the cramped patio set the tone for the

whole backyard, making the rest of it feel crowded as well. For that reason, devoting adequate space to furniture and toys was our first change.

The family was equally surprised to hear that the unrelieved expanse of lawn was actually making the backyard look *smaller*. This is because our eyes have a tendency to foreshorten a space that is flat and monochromatic. Simply expanding was not the best approach. Instead, we changed the lawn's shape to a curvier one, allowing us to add more plants closer to the patio. This not only broke up the overwhelming section of grass, but offered the happy bonus of creating a much more attractive view from the patio.

Finally, we explored the idea of facilitating play in other ways besides providing a lawn. Adding a flat, curving pathway around the lawn's perimeter created a track for bikes, trikes, and games, while breaking up the space so that it was better proportioned. Although these changes were very different than what the homeowners initially thought they wanted, the result was a dynamic, inviting garden that could be used in multiple ways.

Your design should include
space for the activities you
enjoy, like a comfortable
lounge chair for reading or
relaxing.

Defining realistic goals is critical to creating lifestyle spaces. If you are contemplating changes to your yard, you may already have a list of the features you think your new garden should include. But amassing too many elements can quickly lead to what I like to call the "thingy" garden. A typical, modest-sized, urban or suburban backyard has room for only so much. To be shown in their best light, these yards need a little breathing room.

Beginning with a lifestyle-based approach will help you maximize the usable space, which in turn means you and your family will enjoy your backyard more thoroughly. Since my goal with this book is to teach you how to be your own designer, think of this chapter as our first consultation. Learning to define and communicate goals in a meaningful way will help you explain what you are trying to achieve — whether it's to contractors, garden professionals, or even your own family!

Designers refer to this process of gathering information about a new landscape's requirements as the design program. For large and complex gardens, determining the program is an essential first step. But even a simple design for a tiny backyard will be more successful if a program is established before any actual design work begins. Remember, the essence of a lifestyle garden is creating a space that reflects you and those who will use your garden in as many ways as possible. It sounds easy, but I know firsthand it can be surprisingly difficult! Trusting in the three Ws and what they say about how you live keeps things simple and reveals the essential components of your ideal garden.

What Will You Be Doing in the Garden?

A lot of glossy magazines and online media outlets present gardens as belonging to specific design styles, such as cottage or contemporary, so we feel a certain pressure to create something elaborate or with a cohesive selection of plants. Most of us, however, are simply interested in crafting a garden that reflects, accommodates, and enhances our time at home, one that encourages us to use the space we have.

To create a garden that responds to your true needs, the first step is to figure out what kind of activities you realistically plan on doing in your new backyard. You might think, "But my needs are straightforward, like a deck with a table and some

Containers with a mix of culinary herbs and flowers are both beautiful and practical located close to a barbecue.

chairs. What's that got to do with my lifestyle?" While it may sound surprising, even something as seemingly simple as a deck needs some forethought to be successful. A layout that works well for reading and relaxing, for instance, will look quite different than one that is used mainly for dining and entertaining.

Here's a specific example. When clients tell me they want a barbecue island or outdoor kitchen included in their design, I ask these questions:

- How frequently do you cook outside?
- Do you grill year-round?
- Are most meals family only, or do you entertain regularly?
- How elaborate is a typical menu?

Why do these details matter? If a family grills year-round, providing a barbecue with some protection from the elements (or at least locating it near the kitchen door) is important. Likewise, someone who prepares more elaborate meals will require more prep space than the cook who occasionally flips burgers on a sunny afternoon. Questions like these are not only important for space planning in a small area, but for budgeting as well. It makes sense to allocate the highest percentage of your budget to elements that will play a central role in how the garden is enjoyed.

Planting vegetables in Woolly Pockets is a great space-saving strategy.

Enhancing your garden experience

Understanding how you will spend time in your backyard garden also helps identify other design elements that can add to your appreciation of the garden. To continue the example of the backyard barbecuer, I might suggest placing a big pot of herbs or a dwarf fruit tree nearby, if the grill is manned by a serious cook. Not only does this put fresh ingredients within easy reach, it's an inexpensive yet thoughtful touch that reflects your interests. Including simple but useful or meaningful details is one of the best ways to create a garden uniquely your own.

A smaller footprint may mean there isn't room for your entire wish list of features, so focus on creating space for activities instead of objects. More important, considering the "how" encourages a creative approach to doing more with less. For example, if you want vegetables in your landscape but lack the room for a dedicated raised bed, don't jettison the idea of growing your own edible plants. Explore some of the many clever systems now widely available for planting vertically on walls or fences, such as Woolly Pockets. Veggies and herbs can also be mixed with ornamentals in the ground or in pots.

While there is really no right or wrong to garden design if your finished garden makes you happy, over time I've noticed several trends in my clients' satisfaction levels with particular features of their installed, finished landscapes. Regardless of how you plan to spend time in your backyard, elements that emphasize qualities unique to the outdoors will enhance any garden activity.

Water features. One classic example that many homeowners enjoy year after year is a water feature. Not only does such an addition infuse a garden with movement and sound, but because flowing water attracts birds, butterflies, and other beneficial visitors, it also brings a garden to life. However, concerns about maintenance or safety issues (if young children are present) can prompt homeowners to shy away from including a water element in their design. A good compromise solution is to choose an attractive urn or container as an alternative. If in time you decide a water feature would add to your outdoor experience, simply convert the existing urn.

Hardscapes. Unless you are attracted to a strongly contemporary look that revolves around man-made materials like concrete, including some natural hardscape materials helps connect a garden to the natural environment. This is particularly true for those who think of their backyards as a refuge from the day-to-day grind, where they can escape to unwind. Depending on your budget, this can be as expansive as using flagstone as your primary paving material, or as simple as nestling landscape rocks and boulders in planting beds. Remember that landscape rock will be partially embedded in the soil and must have enough heft to stand up to the plants nearby, so avoid choosing rocks that are too small. If your landscape will be professionally installed, it is worth the extra effort to visit your contractor's supplier and choose any landscape rock yourself.

Including natural hardscape materials like river rock will keep your garden connected to the natural world.

Standout plants. Unlike the static décor inside your home, a garden is a living, breathing ecosystem. The changes that occur naturally, whether seasonally or over the years, are something to be celebrated. Although most of us reject the maintenance that goes along with a garden full of fussy plants, having one or two plants that stand out from the ordinary is a charming way to give your garden unique character. High-performing plants include not only those with strong seasonal attributes, such as masses of spring flowers or brilliant fall hues, but also multi-functional plants that are both edible and ornamental, or that combine flower color with intoxicating scent.

Minimizing elements that are seldom used

Remember that gardens require maintenance beyond plant care. It's important to be honest with yourself — not only as to what you will be doing in the garden, but regarding how much time you are willing to spend maintaining the elements you introduce. Features requiring intense maintenance to look their best, particularly

below 'Hot Lips' sage (*Salvia microphylla* 'Hot Lips') is an easy-care perennial that blooms over a long season.

if they are in a highly visible area, are often underutilized. This is especially true of things that duplicate functionality, such as outdoor sinks and refrigerators – they are simply a lot easier to clean and maintain indoors. Think about it. Have you ever started planning a party, only to stop because of the effort of getting your house ready? Now imagine if your kitchen had no roof and the windows were always open!

Elements that take up a lot of space but can only be used or showcased on limited occasions or during one season also tend to become eyesores quickly. Fire pits in warmer climates are one example, as are high-maintenance flower beds in colder climates with a short growing season.

Finally, in a modest-sized lot, space is often at a premium. If the goal is to create a backyard you can relax in as comfortably as you can in your family room, avoid hard benches, undersized seating, or essentially anything that makes the backyard less comfortable to be in. Remember, your goal is not to create a magazine vignette, but an outdoor room you and your family will enjoy for years to come.

When Will You Be Outside?

If you are fortunate, you will have the opportunity to enjoy your backyard at various times of the day and evening as well as multiple days of the week. Depending on the weather where you live, your family's schedule, and personal preferences, you will probably tend to be outside more consistently at certain times. In my family, my husband and I make a point of carving an hour out together in the early evenings, as we transition from work to family mode. So I've designed a modest two-person seating area that is shielded from late afternoon sun in spring and summer, with room for just two comfortable chairs.

Of course, every household is different. For families with young children, the backyard probably gets considerable use on weekday afternoons and weekend days. If you work outside the home, your primary time to enjoy your garden might be on mild evenings or weekend afternoons. Knowing when you will spend the most time outdoors will help you design a garden that is at its most comfortable and pleasant when you are most likely to be in it.

Protection from the elements

Factoring in outdoor conditions is an important part of planning your space. This can mean filtering out sun, adding overhead structures that protect from the rain, or even saving room in the budget for outdoor heaters or a fire pit if you enjoy brisk autumn evenings outside. As a bonus, many of these solutions will extend how often the garden is available to you.

In my own hot California climate, protection from the sun is at the top of almost everyone's list. Arbors and pergolas are popular options for providing respite on sweltering summer days, but are more effective at certain times of the day than others. In the middle of the day, when the sun is directly overhead, a pergola does a good job of blocking intense heat. Later in the afternoon, however, when the sun's rays shine at an angle, they can slip right under an overhead structure. A strategic grouping of small-scale trees or columnar shrubs with a low, branching pattern on the west side of your patio or yard might compensate. To thwart piercing morning or afternoon sun, attach an outdoor curtain to the arbor's beams. Choose a material that can handle the elements but is flexible enough to roll up easily, such as canvas or bamboo.

Pergolas provide structure to a backyard and protection from hot summer sun.

shrubs for blocking sun

Arbors and pergolas are effective at blocking midday sun, but do nothing to prevent the angled sun of late afternoon and early evening, which otherwise is often the most pleasant time to be in the garden. Look for shrubs or small trees with a medium to dense branching pattern that reaches to the ground, and a profile that is narrow rather than wide. Wide shrubs are impractical in smaller gardens—without constant shearing, their girth eats up too much precious real estate.

Plant	USDA zones	Description
American arborvitae (*Thuja* spp.)	4–9	Similar to cypress trees, but with brighter green foliage, cleaner structure, and more compact size. Ideal for gardens where a somewhat formal appearance is desired.
cape mallow (*Lavatera maritima*)	5–9	Fast-growing cape mallow reaches 10 or 12 feet, making it good option for quickly creating a natural sun barrier. It is also short-lived, so consider planting this as a first line of defense while a more permanent option has a chance to gain height.
purple hopseed bush (*Dodonaea viscosa* 'Atropurpurea')	8–10	Fast growing to 12 to 15 feet tall, narrow, evergreen hopseed bush is an excellent choice both to block sun and create privacy from neighbors. Leaves turn a lovely burgundy-red in winter.
smoke bush (*Cotinus coggygria*)	5–9	The shorter days of fall and winter mean afternoon sun protection is less of an issue then, making deciduous plants such as smoke bush an option. A low-water, easy-care shrub reaching 10 to 15 feet.
'Alphonse Karr' clumping bamboo (*Bambusa multiplex* 'Alphonse Karr')	8–10	A popular choice for screening. Unlike invasive bamboos that spread by sending out underground runners, 'Alphonse Karr' is a clumping bamboo. Can reach 20 feet or more, but easily maintained at a lower height.
'Bright 'N Tight' Carolina laurel (*Prunus caroliniana* 'Bright 'N Tight')	7–11	With its dense, evergreen foliage, Carolina laurel maintains an excellent defense against hot, afternoon sun. Its smaller size compared to many similarly dense shrubs—only 8 to 10 feet high and 3 to 6 feet wide—minimizes pruning chores.

clockwise, from top left
American arborvitae, cape mallow, smoke bush, 'Bright 'N Tight' Carolina laurel, 'Alphonse Karr' clumping bamboo, purple hop-seed bush

Plan your garden to be at its best whatever time of the year you expect to spend the most time outside.

In parts of the country that enjoy warm summer rain, an overhead structure with a solid roof will allow you to relax in your garden even during a shower. A space that is also partially enclosed on the sides, such as a gazebo, will provide additional protection. If rain is not as common in your area, a less permanent solution might be a better option. Pop-up cabanas can be recruited for as long as they are needed, whether that is a day or a season, then packed out of the way. Add a string of party lights, and a cabana like this creates an instant outdoor dining room – and the perfect excuse to move your next dinner party outside.

Seasonality

In addition to considering the times of day you are likely to be outside, think about the times of year. For most of us – unless you live in winter-warm climates common in some parts of the Plains and southern states, for example – this is when our gardens are the perfect mix of not too hot and not too cold, typically some combination of late spring, summer, and early fall. The more space devoted to living areas, the less space will be available for plants. For that reason, I like to emphasize plants

This woodland garden shows off the beauty of a Northeast spring.

below The sweetly scented flowers of star jasmine (*Trachelospermum jasminoides*) bloom over an extended period.

that will be putting on their best show during the time of year the garden is in most use. Plants that bloom for two or more seasons and those with colorful or texturally interesting foliage top my list for temperate gardens.

In areas with more extreme seasons, be thoughtful in choosing plants that highlight the garden when you will be most available to enjoy it. For example, when choosing a vine for its scent, I am more likely to select star jasmine (*Trachelospermum jasminoides*), which blooms in warmer gardens on and off throughout the summer, rather than pink jasmine (*Jasminum polyanthum*), which provides only three to four weeks of intense scent in early spring—when the temperature is generally too cool to spend extended time outdoors. Be thoughtful at the nursery, and don't pop the first pretty plant you see into your cart. Take the time to research whether the brilliant blooms or delicious scent you are enjoying will last more than a few short weeks.

If you are in a colder climate, consider a more encompassing approach, and perhaps include a few spring showstoppers or late winter bulbs, even if summer will be your garden's high season. After months of snow, nothing is more cheerful than the first signs of new life right outside your backdoor.

A mix of furniture sizes makes a patio comfortable for adults and kids alike.

Who Will Be with You?

The makeup of most households changes over time. When putting together your program, understanding who will be using the space, both now and as your family expands or shrinks, will ensure that the investment you make in a new landscape today will serve your family's needs well into the future.

If there will only be one or two people using the garden, less space can be allocated to seating. Designing a space for just a few users can also make it easier to find room for more than one seating area. Consider devoting one patio, or portion of a patio, to a dining table and creating a separate area for conversation, reading, or relaxing. Just remember to leave enough space for comfortable furniture! Cushioned seats you can sink into, rocking chairs, or a space with room for a couple of lounge chairs are more likely to be used on a regular basis than a cute but spindly bistro set.

Family time

In addition to dining, large families need space dedicated to play. This may mean lawn, but other surfaces can also accommodate play, such as gravel or gold fines (also known as decomposed granite or DG). If your yard is quite small and there is a neighborhood park close by, don't waste space on a swing set or a patch of lawn that will be too tiny for most kids' games. Dedicate garden space to creative play instead, such as a sandbox, a children's garden, or a craft area.

Planning for younger children also means taking safety into consideration. Water features should be avoided unless they are specifically designed to eliminate the risk of drowning. Using an in-ground reservoir or filling the majority of an above-ground reservoir with gravel is one way to accomplish this. You can also choose a simple birdbath over running water. If you are planning a primary play space, situate it to be visible from a window, making it easier to keep kids in sight while you're indoors.

If your children or grandchildren are very young, do not choose plants with berries or flowers that are poisonous if ingested. (An internet search of "poisonous

You don't need space for a dedicated play structure—opportunities for active play can be integrated throughout the backyard.

Play it safe in gardens
where young children will
be—choose water features
without an above-ground
reservoir.

plants" will bring up lists for different USDA zones.) The website 1stinflowers.com
breaks common plants into categories such as those that cause rashes, those that
cause upset stomachs, and flowers and plants that cause serious conditions—visit
http://www.1stinflowers.com/articles/poisonous-plants-for-children.html.

Consider the comfort of family members or friends with allergies as well. Choosing plants carefully can help entice them outdoors even in high-pollen seasons. Many
all-male tree cultivars have become popular as they are more likely to be litter free,
but unfortunately, they tend to produce much higher levels of pollen. Instead, opt for
a tried-and-true performer such as a crape myrtle (*Lagerstroemia* spp.). Available in a
range of sizes and spring or summer flower color, tolerant of both heat and humidity,
and not a heavy producer of airborne pollen, there are multiple reasons this lovely
tree is popular throughout the country. Another plant category to use sparingly if
allergies are an issue is ornamental grasses. They have become landscape superstars
recently, but unfortunately can cause hay fever. If you like their graceful look and
want to incorporate them into your garden, consider grass-like plants that mimic the

fine, narrow foliage, such as mat rush (*Lomandra* spp.) or flax lily (*Dianella* spp.).

Unless you or a family member is allergic to bees, however, there is no need to avoid the flowers that attract them, such as common yarrow (*Achillea* spp.) and catmint (*Nepeta* spp.). Bees are not aggressive and are necessary pollinators that keep both your garden and the neighborhood around you healthy and productive. Remember, many of the plants that attract desirable garden visitors like birds and butterflies draw honeybees as well, so you can't have one without the other.

As all parents know, having kids requires you to check your perfectionist tendencies at the door. I encourage clients to be realistic about the toys, trikes, and assorted detritus that children (and their adults) inevitably leave strewn around a yard. Despite the impression given by the perfect photos in glossy home and garden magazines, gardens are for people, and most of us don't live a photo-op lifestyle on a daily basis. Make sure attractive storage, whether it's a small shed on the side of the house or all-weather toy chests that can double as deck or patio tables, are part of your plan.

top Unless someone in the family is allergic, there is no need to avoid plants that attract bees.

bottom A shed can be both decorative and practical as a storage solution for smaller gardens.

Planning for pets

If you have pets, take their needs into consideration. For dogs, particularly those left alone outdoors during the day, the most important thing to include is a shady spot. If your canine likes to hollow out a cool patch in the dirt, leave his or her favorite digging area unplanted – don't hope to change your pet's behavior by planting over such places. If your pet is very well-behaved, also consider adding a dedicated potty area filled with gravel.

Many canines have guard dog instincts, and fret if they are unable to walk the perimeter of their yard. Even in a small garden, try to include a continuous pathway around and through most of the garden. This doesn't need to be paved or fancy – just leaving a narrow walking space through each part of the garden can be enough. And dogs like play areas, too! A raised bed filled with sand or gravel will encourage your pet to dig, chew, or play in a designated area if you keep it stocked with a few favorite toys.

Friends and guests

If you entertain frequently, think about how often you realistically host guests, as well as the size of typical get-togethers. If you expect to host more than four to six for meals on a regular basis, make sure the size of the patio or deck can accommodate guests sitting, standing, and mingling comfortably. On the other hand, if you only entertain larger groups occasionally, it might be better to have a flexible plan that lets you seat crowds in a pinch. Just as a big family gathering at the holidays means pressing temporary tables and chairs into service, it may make sense to keep extra folding chairs and tables in storage, and bring them out only when necessary. As homeowners have extended the ways they spend time in their gardens, the outdoor furniture industry has kept pace. It's easy to find furniture pieces such as drink trolleys that can be wheeled from one part of the garden to another, then stored away when not in use. Dining tables with leaves stored inside are popular for expanding seating from six to a dinner party of ten or twelve.

Understandably, once the decision is made to upgrade a backyard, most of us want to jump in and get started immediately. But taking time to thoroughly identify what you really want to get out of your space, and being open to examining your own assumptions, is a crucial first step toward creating a truly successful, livable garden. The more you focus on enhancing your lifestyle rather than simply installing a list of things, the more you will truly enjoy spending time in your garden.

Pets are family members, too. Keep their needs in mind when planning your garden.

design templates for modest-size yards

Designing a new garden from scratch is a wonderfully rewarding creative process. When you first settle in to begin planning each element of your garden, however, staring at a blank piece of paper while waiting for inspiration to strike can be a little intimidating. If you've been taking photos of your neighbors' yards, browsing design sites, or trolling the local garden centers in search of ideas, you've probably absorbed so many great ones that you're not sure where to start. To avoid design paralysis, the trick is to break up the process into a series of manageable tasks, while keeping a few basic guidelines in mind as your ideas begin to take shape.

With the right planning, small gardens can still provide room for an active, outdoor lifestyle.

Once you've outlined your lifestyle goals, the next logical step is taking an inventory of your existing backyard to determine which aspects are working and which are in need of an overhaul. This process will be most successful if you follow a simple hierarchy – begin with the primary living spaces, structures, and pathways; then move on to plants; and end with accessories.

Assessing your backyard in this order can take discipline. Because plants contribute so much to a garden's character and uniqueness, there is a natural tendency to jump right in with plant selection. Now, there's nothing wrong with having a passion for plants and wanting to choose them wisely. It's great to love cottage gardens or to want a space that is filled with color. But save all those wonderful ideas for later and instead begin your design by laying out the garden's permanent elements. Where will the patio or deck be? Where will pathways be required? If there's a lawn, where does it go? How about the planting beds? (Never mind what goes in the planting beds yet!)

Three Keys to Successful Yards

While there are myriad ways a backyard can be designed to reflect the owners' aesthetic taste and lifestyle goals, designs that stand the test of time have three key factors in common.

Scale and proportion. Because each element in a backyard is part of the whole, proportion and scale are important to make the space feel balanced.

Circulation. Good planning allows us to move intuitively through a backyard. Attention to circulation ensures that patios, decks, and walkways are easily maneuvered and desirable views remain unobstructed.

Comfort. Finally, all design decisions should be made with comfort in mind, whether that means adequate protection from the hot summer sun or cozy furniture that invites you to sit back and unwind.

As you work through practical design decisions like patio size and plant choices, occasionally pause and revisit these three guiding principles to make sure your design remains on track.

Scale and proportion

Scale refers to the way the garden's elements relate to a fixed object. For a backyard design, that fixed object is you. In other words, when you enter a garden, do the size and shape of the garden's various components feel relatable? A privacy screen of 50-foot-tall Italian cypress looming over a small garden might make you feel claustrophobic, as if the walls are closing in on you. A more appropriately sized stand of narrow arborvitae (*Thuja* spp.), on the other hand, will still provide privacy while

being relatable on a human scale. Scale is also important when choosing accessories. Small or fragile furniture crowded onto a deck can make us feel large and awkward, like adults trying to fit into a child-sized classroom.

Proportion refers to how the elements of a garden relate, not only to items immediately next to those elements, but to the overall space in general. Proportion can be challenging in small- to average-sized gardens; the pressure to fit everything in means we include elements that are too small to be practical, while other aspects wind up too big. For example, a difficult element to design proportionately in small backyards is a lawn. If you are including lawn as a neutral space for ornamental purposes, by the time patios or decks, paths, and other garden essentials have been added, the space left for lawn is often too small in relation to the surrounding elements. Because hardscape can provide similar calm contrast for surrounding planted beds, you could instead consider wider pathways as a better-proportioned alternative. Conversely, assigning a flat, monochromatic stretch of turf too much space may result in a proportionately oversized lawn, relegating elements with height and mass, such as plants or furniture, to the garden's edges.

When there are no plants or objects to break up a long, open space, a garden is

Introducing level changes helps keep a garden proportionate and adds interest to a small space.

Your design should leave room to easily move through the space.

sapped of visual interest. Introducing a mix of heights – via natural level changes in the topography, built features like pergolas or raised beds, or through planting strategies – combats this.

This vertical aspect of proportion is an important one. It doesn't just address the relationship of flat spaces to surrounding greenery, but also the connection between the plants themselves. In general, avoid placing tall or broad trees in flat areas with nothing to support them or soften their presence. Low-growing lawn or ground cover planted all around can visually strand a tree, disconnecting it from the rest of the garden. Surrounding trees with medium-sized shrubs or perennials helps bridge the proportional gap created when very tall objects shoot up from an unvarying, low understory. The need to keep larger elements in proportion applies to built features and accessories as well. Nestle plants around larger fountains or sculptures, or ensure they are balanced by smaller aspects nearby, such as plants, raised beds, or furniture.

Circulation

The best gardens are a pleasure not only to look at, but to spend time in. Landscape architect Thomas Church's groundbreaking book, *Gardens Are for People*, was written in 1955, but the title's essential premise is still important today, even for the simplest of designs. While sketching out your potential garden, remember that once it is installed it *must* be practical and pleasant to move around in. This means making sure there is enough room to walk comfortably around and between planting beds and other elements. It also means creating circulation patterns that actively pull people through the garden.

For these reasons, as you work on your design, don't lose sight of how the space will be navigated. Begin with the obvious: Where are the garden's exits and entrances? Note all doors and gates and make sure there is an easy and intuitive way to access them. Once your design begins to take shape, keep track of any high-activity areas, such as vegetable gardens or gazebos, and make sure there is a way to reach them, too, whether formally, via a path, or informally, perhaps by walking across a lawn or a patch of ground cover. If the backyard includes planted areas wider than 8 or 10 feet, consider weaving a pathway or a few stepping-stones through the space. Not only is this an effective way to encourage movement throughout the whole garden, it also provides access for maintenance chores. Just as company inside tends to congregate in the kitchen, outdoor guests won't move far from the patio or deck without incentive. Visitors to your garden will enjoy themselves much more if the layout encourages exploration beyond the back door, so make paths obvious and inviting.

Once you've incorporated physical circulation into your plan, consider how other design elements will appear when viewed from several different places in the garden. If your design includes an arbor, for example, will its posts block access to pathways or block key views as you move from one part of the garden to another? Is your patio large enough to hold all your furniture and still leave room to comfortably navigate around it and move chairs in and out? Measure the furniture you have or are planning to buy and create proportionate shapes out of construction paper, then move them around on your design to test their workability. Outside, use landscape paint, garden hoses, twine, or flags to mark the shape and size of the patio or deck to ensure it will be appropriate for your entertaining and dining needs.

Comfort

You should be as comfortable in your backyard as you are in your favorite indoor spaces. Protection from the elements plays a big role in this. Strategies that provide shelter from the sun will keep your garden usable during the hottest days of summer. A well-planned garden goes beyond off-the-shelf shade solutions. While an umbrella or pergola can offer some protection from the sun, neither will cool the environment. Likewise, large expanses of concrete and lawn do little to combat summer heat. That's why it is important to allot generous space for trees and other green and growing things, as in addition to decreasing air temperature by blocking the sun, plants help cool the environment simply by existing. Just as we do, plants "breathe" or transpire, releasing moisture from their leaves into the atmosphere. This process, known as evapotranspiration, helps cool the air, particularly in drier climates where the lack of humidity tends to speed the rate of evaporation. The Environmental Protection Agency estimates that the effects of evapotranspiration can reduce peak summer temperatures from two to nine degrees. Combine this with the cooling effect of shade trees, particularly over non-reflective paving materials, and the shady parts of your garden can be 25 degrees cooler than the surrounding area.

Because temperature is so important, if a large portion of your backyard is exposed, consider making a sun/shade study part of the assessment process. This will allow you to actively track sun patterns, and help you decide where shade structures or trees should be added or removed. To do this, draw a map of your backyard's existing boundaries. (You will need this base map for your landscape design anyway.) Use irrigation flags or other markers such as bricks or large rocks to mark off 2- to 3-foot intervals from east to west across the length or width of your garden. Then, create corresponding lines across your drawing and make multiple copies. Beginning at 8 a.m. on a relatively sunny day and ending whenever the garden is fully in shadow, label each copy with an hour of the day. Every hour that day, check the backyard and use a pencil to show where the garden is shaded on the corresponding copy of the base map. By the end of the day, you will know where your yard is sunny throughout the day, which will greatly improve your ability to design appropriate protection.

Cold is an issue for garden lovers in just about every part of the country as the seasons change, and even warm-weather regions become cooler in the evenings. If space allows, a fire pit can be a great outdoor addition. Depending on your budget and personal tastes, you can have one custom built, or purchase a pit that is prefabricated. Remember that this type of feature will be a visible part of the landscape and most likely serve as a focal point even when not in use, so choose a style in tune with the rest of the garden. Fortunately, fire pits are an increasingly popular landscape feature, and manufacturers have responded with a range of styles, from sleekly sophisticated to charmingly rustic.

The choice between a wood-burning fire pit or one with a gas insert is dependent on several factors. Wood-burning fire pits typically generate more warmth, and just as with an indoor fireplace, the amount of heat they cast can be manipulated. Using wood for fuel creates an intoxicating ambience — crackling flames, sizzling pops, and that unmistakable campfire scent are hard to resist. On a practical note, choose a location away from overhanging tree limbs and vegetation at risk of catching fire. Be aware that some municipalities have restrictions against burning wood; be sure to verify local requirements and guidelines.

Trees do more than add beauty and shade to a garden; they keep a garden cool by releasing moisture through their leaves.

Comparatively speaking, prefabricated gas units are much simpler to enjoy, requiring only the flick of a switch to bring them to life. No need to keep firewood on hand, nor to spend time and energy creating a fire and keeping it fed. Gas won't provide a significant amount of heat, however, and may be a better choice in areas where evenings are warmer or a subtle effect is desired. Regardless of which option you choose, consider a fire pit with a ledge that's at least 12 inches wide. This creates room for plates and glasses, allowing the space to double as a table when extra seating is desirable.

Beyond temperature, comfort should also be top of mind when choosing furniture. Stone benches and wire-framed bistro sets can be attractive focal points, but make sure everyday seating is large and comfortable enough to encourage lingering. I also recommend having a designated space for gardening tools and maintenance paraphernalia—out of sight of the main seating area. It will be much easier to relax in your favorite outdoor chair if the hedge clippers aren't parked nearby, a silent reminder of garden chores.

When designing a new garden, comfort is king! That includes furniture you can sink into.

opposite Adirondack chairs tucked around a simple fire pit create a welcoming place to relax as the sun goes down.

Breaking up a Boxy Backyard

Most small to average-sized gardens are rectangular. The most common backyards I see, both in recent suburban developments and older neighborhoods dominated by ranch houses and bungalows, are shallow and long. The trick to countering the uninspiring rectangle that defines many of our yards is to start with a layout plan that de-emphasizes the boxiness of the space.

Although there are many ways a garden can be laid out, for a typical suburban backyard, it's better to stick with one of two general categories: organic gardens whose lines are built around curves and meandering spaces, or a backyard laid out along the more structured lines of rectangles, squares, and circles.

Setting up a series of garden rooms is an attractive, efficient way to organize a space and a good option whether you lean toward an organic space or a more linear one. If your backyard is only average sized, you might think transforming it into a series of separate spaces will make it feel smaller, but in fact, the opposite is true. A layout based on one large patio surrounded by lawn and garden lacks interest, which stops the eye (and the feet) from moving through and exploring the space. The result is a backyard that feels cramped and inadequate. In contrast, a garden separated into different areas, even subtly, creates a sense of multiple destinations and an overall impression of a larger space.

While it's seldom practical in a small backyard to completely separate one area from another, a series of connected nooks partially separated by mini plant groupings or garden structures brings a touch of mystery and discovery, and results in a garden that feels intimate. This means letting go of traditional notions of planting one long border around the perimeter of the yard and instead interspersing plants and seating areas throughout the space.

A permeable "wall" of bamboo separates one part of the garden from another without blocking it off.

Organic Designs

Gardens based on organic shapes, relying on curves to define the edges of borders, beds, and walkways, are very popular for small city and suburban yards. Plantings and other garden features are generally laid out in an asymmetrical fashion, with plants and other ornaments grouped in odd numbers such as threes, fives, or sevens. This style has broad appeal; the curves offset the hard lines of an already-rectangular space, while also mimicking what we see in nature. After all, shrubs and trees don't plant themselves in rows, and rivers and streams don't flow in a straight line.

The patio or deck is usually the most prominent element in a residential yard, and therefore a logical place to begin designing an organic layout. A gracefully curved patio creates a strong center around which a garden can revolve. While surrounding a patio with curved planting beds is a good strategy for softly transitioning from hardscaped areas of the yard to planted areas, it also helps suggest room divisions rather than starkly delineating them. Furniture placed near see-through or low plants implies separation, but doesn't create multiple distinct patios the way a clipped hedge or garden wall would.

Keep in mind that choosing an organic design style doesn't necessarily mean that everything in the garden must be curved. A curved deck surrounded by a curving lawn and curved planting beds can be too much of a good thing — consider balancing curves with some straight lines. Avoid "curve competition" by extending the straight lines of the house farther into the garden with a rectangular deck, allowing the surrounding curves of lawns, planting beds, and pathways to take center stage.

When multiple curves converge, they can unintentionally create undesirable acute angles, that is, narrow, pointed places where intersecting hardscape or lawn borders create awkward, arrow-shaped planting areas. Spaces like this are a challenge as they are difficult to plant in, and typical garden bed fillers like mulch and stone tend not to stay put. Of course, sometimes including a spot like this is unavoidable. In those instances, ground covers are an ideal solution. Those with small leaves that are easily trimmed, such as creeping thyme (*Thymus* spp.) and blue star creeper (*Laurentia fluviatilis*), tuck neatly into spaces like this without obscuring the lines of the garden.

If you opt to make curves the centerpiece of your design, be bold! Curves should be strong and clearly defined so they look intentional. Steer clear of meandering, wavy lines — these make it look like you created the yard without a real plan in mind.

Curving designs often result in acute angles that are difficult to plant. In this case, a ground cover such as pachysandra is an ideal solution.

opposite The curved shapes of the patio tile and raised beds in this garden counteract the squareness of the surrounding walls.

template 1

transform a narrow backyard

When we moved to Northern California in the mid-nineties, my husband and I settled on a brand-new house because we loved its interiors. Unfortunately, what came with it was a small, 1000-square-foot backyard filled with plain dirt and an unattractive wooden retaining wall. Over the ensuing years, we gradually transformed it into an intimate jewel box garden that's become our favorite place to relax, eat, and entertain. Defying the common wisdom that small spaces need to be manicured and minimalist to be successful, we proceeded to stuff the beds with lushly blooming plants and to blanket the patio with containers. We even transformed the fences, adding wooden panels painted in a range of colors for additional layers of interest.

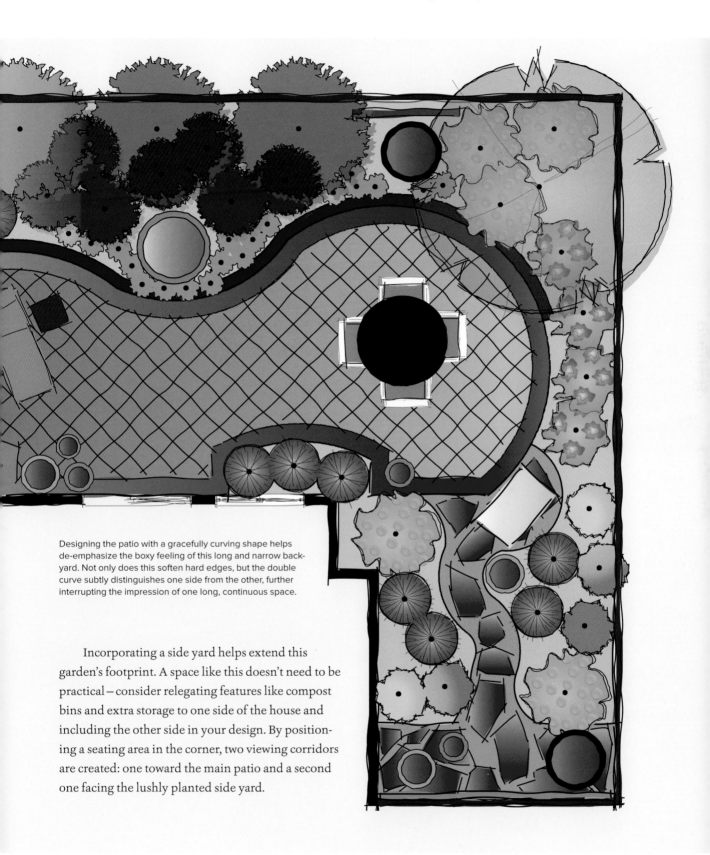

Designing the patio with a gracefully curving shape helps de-emphasize the boxy feeling of this long and narrow back-yard. Not only does this soften hard edges, but the double curve subtly distinguishes one side from the other, further interrupting the impression of one long, continuous space.

Incorporating a side yard helps extend this garden's footprint. A space like this doesn't need to be practical – consider relegating features like compost bins and extra storage to one side of the house and including the other side in your design. By position-ing a seating area in the corner, two viewing corridors are created: one toward the main patio and a second one facing the lushly planted side yard.

opposite top A kidney-shaped patio that anchors the gardens is key to breaking up the long, dreary fence line. The patio also acts as negative space that reins in surrounding greenery.

opposite bottom A table for dining on one side and a lounge chair for relaxing on the other establish two garden destinations in a relatively small area.

left A lavender-colored rose trellis echoes the color of nearby containers and flowers.

above left A fountain in the patio's curve creates a shared focal point that ties together the separate destinations for dining and relaxing.

above Color can be repeated throughout a garden for dramatic effect in simple ways such as seat cushions—not just with plants.

opposite Besides complementing containers and plantings, these painted panels ensure the backyard will be colorful all year round, even when plants are not in bloom.

below left Smaller plants like hens and chicks (*Echeveria ×imbricata*) and 'Gold Strike' lily-of-the-Nile (*Agapanthus* 'Gold Strike') are tucked near seating areas, where their sculptural beauty can be admired up close.

below right By surrounding the patio with planting beds and layering plants lushly, this backyard's small space becomes an advantage, as both seating areas feel cozily wrapped in garden.

above left and right Containers scattered throughout the garden draw the eye and create a sense of discovery, an important consideration in smaller gardens, which rely on multiple layers of interest to keep them visually stimulating.

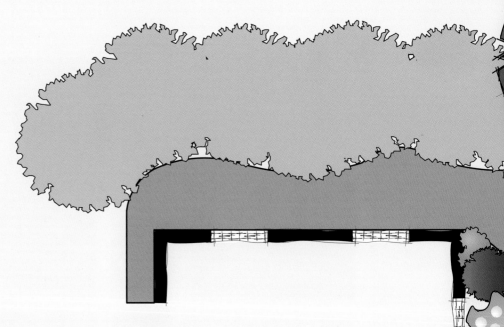

template 2

use curves to tie an awkward space together

New construction created a challenging sloped space that was virtually unusable on this upstate New York property. The homeowners, who are part-time residents, craved a simple retreat to serve as a cozy oasis amid the surrounding woodlands. To render the garden more usable and to create a sense of enclosure, designer Catharine Cooke utilized cut-and-fill terracing techniques to divide the yard into two distinct levels. Because the house is only occupied for part of the year, she and her design partner, Ian Gribble, chose plants requiring minimal maintenance to replace the patchy, sun-starved lawn. Informal gravel edged with easy-care plants boasting lush, mounding foliage define this garden's curves.

   The choice of organic materials like stacked fieldstone for the retaining wall and gravel for the patio and pathways is a nod to the wooded slopes that surround the garden; such materials help tie the yard to the larger landscape. On sloped sites like this one, where rainwater is directed toward the home, choosing a permeable paving material helps ensure good drainage.

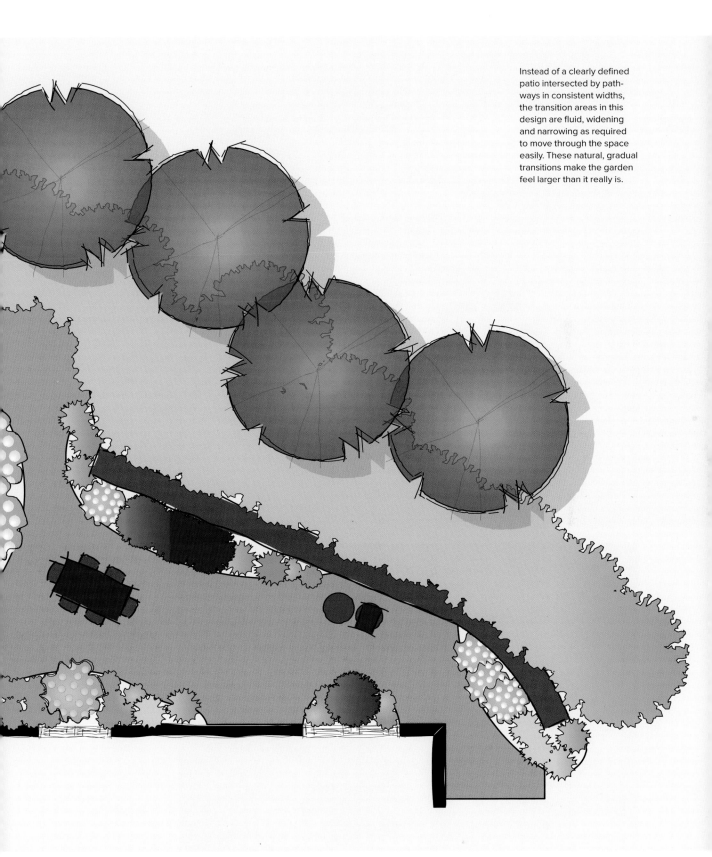

Instead of a clearly defined patio intersected by pathways in consistent widths, the transition areas in this design are fluid, widening and narrowing as required to move through the space easily. These natural, gradual transitions make the garden feel larger than it really is.

opposite top The addition of a gently curved stacked stone retaining wall creates a level patio wide enough for seating, as well as planting beds and a modest barbecue. In a narrow space like this, opting for low ground cover like pachysandra rather than a mix of taller plants stops the slope from looming over the patio below, and keeps the focus on patio plantings.

opposite bottom In smaller spaces, borders don't need to be sharply defined with concrete banding or mow strips. Shrubs and perennials with leaves that rest gently against the edges of seating nooks and pathways result in a graceful yet informal effect. Using only one paving material keeps this garden feeling unified and uncluttered.

above The understated plant palette of whites and golds combined with rustic, neutral furniture results in a restful garden that emphasizes texture and form over bright colors. Plants, including hostas and hydrangeas, shine over a long season with minimal maintenance.

left Sunny flowers such as yellow wax bells (*Kirengeshoma palmata*) provide a cheerful color echo to nearby gold-leafed plants.

left bottom The glowing foliage of Japanese forest grass (*Hakonechloa macra* 'Aureola') adds a burst of sunshine to this shady space.

Geometric Designs

The gardens of the General-
ife in Granada, Spain, are a
classic example of geometric design.

Designing a garden with strong lines and geometric shapes such as rectangles, circles, and triangles has been a staple of landscape design for thousands of years. The Achaemenid Persian empire pioneered this approach by creating enclosed, rectangular gardens organized around a central water source. Their iconic paradise gardens have influenced the world of landscape design ever since, from the cloisters of medieval Europe to the elegant estates of the French and Italian aristocracy during the Renaissance.

One of the benefits of designing a garden with rectilinear shapes versus meandering curves is that it uses space efficiently and is easy for visitors to "read" and use. An intricately curved patio, for example, can potentially wind up with areas that are too small or awkward to use. Gardens built around strong lines can also be particularly pleasing when viewed from a distance or from a second-story window or balcony, as the overall composition will stand out clearly and immediately.

Geometric designs laid out in a formal pattern often rely on a central axis, sometimes supported by a cross axis. The central axis is essentially a straight, prominent line created by a patio, deck, path, or even a pool, that terminates in a focal point to pull the eye through the space. This is an effective way to both guide the visitor into the garden, and to make a shorter space seem longer. In a smaller garden, the central axis may not be a pathway; centering the main entrance or view into the garden on a focal point such as a water feature or specimen tree will have a similar effect.

The planting design that accompanies a geometric design can either reinforce a formal appearance or work to soften it. Arranging plants in pairs or in even-numbered, symmetrical groups focuses attention on any straight lines within a garden. That is because when the eye sees an even-numbered grouping, the tendency is to divide the objects into pairs, in turn emphasizing what lies between. Flanking a view or pathway with symmetrical plantings will create a more formal appearance and is an effective way to draw attention to favored garden elements. Conversely, if you gravitate toward clean, modern lines but want to add a note of informality, plant in odd numbers and resist lining plants up in rigid formation.

Geometric design is a good choice for those who favor a modern look and minimalist style. Plants often assume a less prominent role, and may be chosen for their architectural quality or for their ability to mass well, thereby complementing the strong lines of the hardscape design. When the hardscape plays the central role, material choice is key. To successfully create this type of clean, contemporary landscape for a home, complement concrete with natural materials such as stone or wood stained in rich colors to keep the space from feeling cold or sterile.

Gardens designed around strong shapes are particularly attractive when viewed from above.

Although a geometric garden design style is most often associated with formal or contemporary gardens, it is actually a successful organizing principle in informal gardens as well. Careful material selection, plant choices, and the softening effect of a few non-linear elements are excellent ways to squeeze more livable space from an average-sized lot.

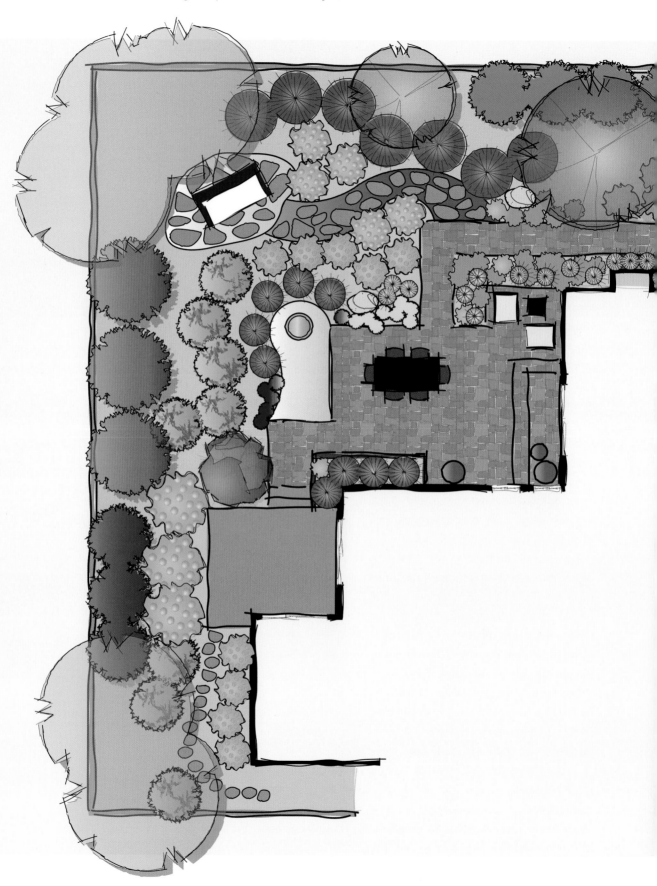

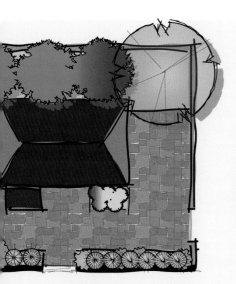

By laying out the primary patios and pathways as a series of interconnected rectangles that create planting pockets throughout, this garden is characterized by inviting patios and nooks, multiple views, and a warm, welcoming ambience.

template 3

modern lines mix with lush plantings

This inviting California backyard manages to pack multiple seating areas and engaging views into a modest suburban space without any of it feeling cramped. The homeowners' goals included a garden that would feel intimate and appropriate for their family of two, while also being large enough for entertaining extended family and hosting fundraising events. As active gardeners and plant lovers, the decision to replace lawn with low-water shrubs, grasses, and perennials was an easy one.

above The gracious scale of the primary patio and steps leading from the dining room to the outdoors creates just enough room to tuck in a few comfortable chairs.

opposite Advance planning is key when designing a garden with a small footprint. The central space is the main patio, which is large enough for both family dining and entertaining.

right and right bottom Effective space planning needs to encompass more than just living spaces. Practical considerations, such as the location of trash receptacles, barbecue grills, and gardening tools should also be a part of the initial design development process.

above This intimate seating area tucked under mature redwoods (*Sequoia sempervirens*) away from the main patio not only provides a one- or two-person retreat, it encourages people to move throughout the garden during larger gatherings, keeping any one area from becoming crowded.

opposite top Keeping secondary pathways narrow allows plants to intermingle with hardscape throughout the garden. Emphasizing plants over lawn is an easy way to bring more color and coziness to a backyard. A warm palette of green and gold foliage with spots of blue is complemented by splashes of coral flowers.

opposite left Including more than one seating area in a backyard is not just about arbitrarily creating different places to sit—viewing a garden from multiple perspectives allows the garden to be experienced in a variety of ways, which increases your ability to enjoy it.

opposite right Homeowners sometimes shy away from a strongly geometric garden plan, for fear it will end up cold or overly formal. A way to combat that is to create one strong or meandering curve as a counterpoint to the more rigid shapes elsewhere in the yard. This winding flagstone path interplanted with fragrant creeping thyme (*Thymus* spp.) keeps the garden from feeling too formal.

opposite In addition to being a destination itself, the Adirondack bench on this tiny rear patio acts as a focal point when the backyard is entered via the side gate, pulling visitors into the space.

top Located toward the center of the garden, the water feature is visible from all seating areas, as well as most windows of the house. Its clean lines allow it to stand out from the surrounding plants, making it a simple yet effective focal point that ties the various seating areas together.

center The lightly scented coral flowers of repeat-blooming 'Voodoo' hybrid tea roses (*Rosa* 'Voodoo') are a brilliant foil to the celadon-colored water feature.

bottom To keep the space lively, a water source is included to attract birds, bees, and butterflies to the garden.

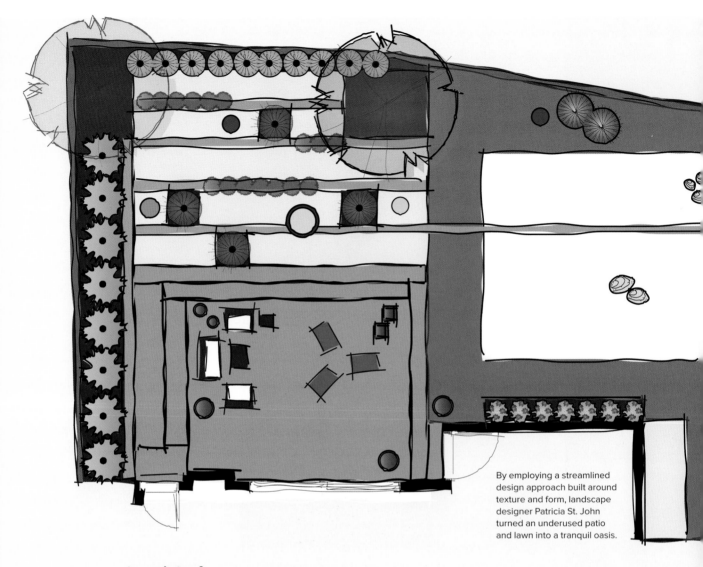

By employing a streamlined design approach built around texture and form, landscape designer Patricia St. John turned an underused patio and lawn into a tranquil oasis.

template 4

keep it simple for a calming retreat

A mid-century modern ranch home's backyard combines the serenity of the East with the relaxed, outdoor lifestyle of the West. This renovation began with a strong vision, as the homeowner was looking for an easy-to-maintain garden, evocative of the simple, understated elegance he associated with his childhood home in Shanghai. Besides being a haven for the family, the garden is regularly pressed into service as an entertaining space and needed to accommodate up to twenty guests at a time. A 14-foot folding glass door separating the interior from the garden made it imperative that the two spaces flow together and provide attractive views of the garden from the inside.

below Natural materials like pebble and gravel alternate with thoughtfully placed rectangles of concrete and planted squares, contrasting color and texture to create a living work of Mondrian-esque art. A narrow band of black Mexican pebble connects the Zen garden to the main garden.

bottom The large deck is composed of a material similar in tone to the dining room's floor, seamlessly connecting indoors and outside. An airy patio cover made from white shade sails provides protection from the sun without closing off views.

A gracious deck is expansive
enough for entertaining.
Intimate groupings of
furniture make it cozy for
smaller gatherings as well.
When additional seating is
required, a dining table fitted
with castors is easily rolled
onto the deck.

top Plants and ornaments are kept to a minimum and placed to highlight the bold hardscape patterns. Finely textured ornamental grasses such as cape rush (*Chondropetalum tectorum*), mat rush (*Lomandra longifolia* 'Breeze'), and Berkeley sedge (*Carex divulsa*), along with smooth-sided bowls and concrete orbs, serve as soft accents to rectilinear surfaces.

center Removing several fence panels and replacing them with see-through screening opens up additional views of the creek that runs behind the home.

bottom The inclusion of Zen-garden elements such as a raked gravel meditation plot adds the calming illusion of water to this otherwise dry garden.

Adapting an Existing Garden

The previous case studies involved new gardens that were designed from scratch; however, the same design strategies are effective even if you are only making changes to a portion of your backyard. The core principles of using strong shapes in a consistent, repeated pattern and weaving planting beds throughout a space rather than relegating them to the outer perimeter of the yard can be used to guide any layout plan.

Choosing plants and hardscapes that can blend elements of a revamped garden with an existing garden does take a little finesse, but there are basic guiding principles to follow here as well. With plants, incorporate some of the same varieties you already have across the entire yard or space. Rather than planting merely a young version of the old garden, consider making space in mature beds for some of the plants chosen for the new beds. Choosing some small, fast-growing plants that will fill in quickly in both the old and new beds will make the garden feel cohesive in the shortest amount of time. Plant breeders and growers have introduced an astonishing wealth of new plant varieties in the last fifteen years, so if you started your original garden longer ago than that, prepare to be pleasantly surprised by how relatively easy it will seem to rejuvenate a dated plant palette with ornamental grasses, long-flowering perennials, or succulents.

Hardscape additions take forethought to integrate, as over time patios and pathways may have become faded or stained, or the original materials may no longer be available. If budget constraints or lack of availability mean new materials will be introduced, consider using borders of a new material to tie spaces together. For example, if the existing patio is concrete and the new pathways or patio will be flagstone, simply add a flagstone border to the existing patio. Choosing a new material in a similar color or pattern to the existing material can also be an effective fix. Informal pathways of a similarly colored, irregular-shaped flagstone, for example, are an attractive complement to a bluestone patio set in a rectangular pattern.

If your patio is concrete and you want to change its shape or size, be aware that it will be impossible to exactly match the color of the existing concrete because of wear, fading, and other consequences of time. In this situation, rather than removing the old hardscape and starting from scratch, a budget-friendly option is to use the current concrete patio as a foundation for a new flagstone or tile patio. To extend the patio, pour new concrete and create the desired new shape — since it ultimately will be covered, it doesn't matter that the new color is not a match for the old. If part of the old patio needs to be removed to accommodate the design (to turn a rectangular patio into a curvy one, for example), use a saw cutter. Once the new patio has cured, flagstone, tile, or brick veneer can be mortared right over the top. This is much less costly than removing all the existing concrete and starting from scratch.

opposite top This original side patio was square and unadorned.

opposite bottom Instead of removing the patio and starting from scratch, the homeowners chose a budget-friendly approach. A saw cutter was used to reshape the edges, which were then tiled over with flagstone.

streamlined design

The word "streamlined" is more likely to bring to mind an image of a sleek, powerful sports car or a living room decorated with minimalist, ultramodern furniture than a suburban backyard. But the word can also apply to garden design. Streamlined, for our purposes, simply means designing efficiently and effectively.

A backyard is efficient when you have organized it to hold distinct spaces for all the essential garden elements you identified during the initial planning phase. Since space is at a premium in small or average-sized backyards, taking advantage of every square inch is crucial to creating an outdoor area you will be able to use well and often.

Instead of one continuous space, a patio is divided into two separate living areas, each attractively bordered by garden.

This patio is large enough to easily accommodate outdoor dining for eight.

A garden is effective when it lures you in. Even when all the functional elements have been included in the design, if a backyard is not a pleasure to spend time in or comfortable to navigate, if pleasing focal points or views are not created or enhanced, then the design is not an effective one. Maintenance also plays a role. Choosing plants and hardscape materials that are attractive, durable, and not overly fussy frees more time for simply enjoying being in the garden without feeling like outstanding chores must be tackled.

Designing a garden usually happens in phases. Once you have the basic layout established, the next step is to refine it, and that means optimizing each element. Even if you are only looking to make upgrades to a few portions of your garden, the guidelines for patios, pathways, and stairs outlined below will help you make sure the new design is as functional as possible.

Patios and Decks

Because decks and patios are the centerpiece of most backyards, efficiency and effectiveness are crucial to choosing the location of these elements and determining their shape and size. The most important consideration sounds simple, but it's worth thinking through: make sure the feature is large enough. This goes beyond blocking out space to accommodate typical elements like tables and barbecues. You must also plan for enough space *around* these items so they can be comfortably enjoyed. With dining tables, a general rule of thumb is to leave at least 2 feet of clearance around the perimeter. In fact, it is not uncommon to see furniture arranged with about this much space in design magazine photos — this can be misleading, however, as gardens are often staged to optimize a photographic angle. Unless you are very short on space, I recommend stretching beyond this to a minimum clearance of 4 feet. This leaves enough room for chairs to be comfortably pushed back from the table, a particularly important consideration if the patio's edge is uneven or higher than the surrounding area. Dining and socializing outdoors should be comfortable for guests — extra space ensures they aren't constantly in fear of tipping a chair off the patio's edge or bumping a neighbor. Keep in mind that a patio or deck adjacent to the back door must also function as a pass-through corridor to and from the garden, even when the patio itself is not in use. Extra clearance means you will be able to navigate easily. This is less of a consideration for smaller, secondary patios, which don't generally see a large volume of traffic.

Your design must address practical and aesthetic considerations as well. If you'll be using the patio during the day, protection from the sun is an important factor. For small backyards, privacy screening from neighbors is probably a key consideration. A pergola can partially accomplish both of these goals, as can planting for privacy and protection, whether as a stand-alone solution or in addition to a shade structure. Choosing attractive and functional plants for these pragmatic purposes is an opportunity to add another layer of beauty to the garden. Small screening trees and large shrubs, however, should be spaced slightly away from the perimeter of a patio border rather than right up next to the edge. This will avoid making the patio feel crowded and will also preserve prime growing space for smaller perennials and shrubs.

The plants you choose for garden beds adjacent to the patio have the potential to be more than just problem solvers. An important but often overlooked aspect of space planning is creating views and interesting details that catch the eye, and plants can play a starring role. Think about it — when dining out, isn't it nicer to be ushered to a table with a view of a nighttime skyline rather than the sign to the restrooms? Likewise, situating plants and other focal points like water or art features where they can be seen and enjoyed from the patio will greatly increase your enjoyment of the garden. No matter how small your space, there are ways to avoid situating a patio where seating faces utilitarian features like trash cans or compost bins.

moonlight gardens

Determining when you will use the patio the most can help with plant choices. If you expect to use your patio in the early evenings, consider plants popular in moonlight gardens—specifically, those that seem to glow with the fading light of day. Plants with silver or chartreuse-colored leaves or those with light-colored flowers are good choices.

Plant	USDA zones	Description
'Gold Strike' lily-of-the-Nile (*Agapanthus* 'Gold Strike')	6–10	This compact, clumping evergreen boasts strappy foliage striped in bright shades of green and gold. Cheerful blue flowers on 2-foot stems appear in midsummer.
night-blooming jasmine (*Cestrum nocturnum*)	9–10	With its narrow profile, this shrub makes an excellent specimen plant for narrow spaces in warmer climates. The petite, greenish white flowers reflect back the light, but the real attraction is the intoxicating fragrance they bring to an evening garden.
'Jack Frost' Siberian bugloss (*Brunnera macrophylla* 'Jack Frost')	3–9	Silvery, heart-shaped leaves with delicate green veining and margins allow this deciduous perennial to sparkle in low light. Small, pale blue flowers rise above the foliage in spring.
'Bello Grigio' lamb's ears *Stachys* 'Bello Grigio')	4–9	Bright silver leaves make this plant a knockout in a moonlight garden. You'll be tempted to pet its fuzzy leaves every time you walk by. Plant for the brilliant foliage; it does not readily flower.
'Limelight' licorice plant (*Helichrysum petiolare* 'Limelight')	9–11	'Limelight' licorice plant's unusually bright chartreuse leaves not only add subtle glow to moonlit gardens but also contrast attractively with dark green or burgundy-colored plants. Plant in part sun for best color.
white sage (*Salvia apiana*)	8–11	White sage delivers on both foliage and flower color. Large, sword-shaped, silver-white leaves adorn stiffly upright woody stems. Small white blooms that are a magnet for bees appear in spring.

left Moonlight gardens catch evening light—ideal for those who enjoy their garden later in the day.

center, from left 'Gold Strike' lily-of-the-Nile, night-blooming jasmine, 'Bello Grigio' lamb's ears, 'Limelight' licorice plant

bottom, from left 'Jack Frost' Siberian bugloss, white sage

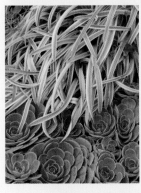

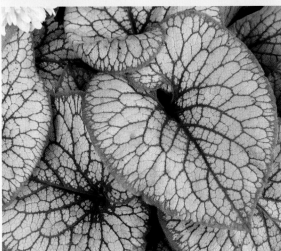

Pathways and Stairs

The material and width you choose for pathways through the garden need to be appropriate to the overall space. Garden pathways are generally grouped into two categories: primary and secondary. Primary pathways are those that lead to an important destination, such as an entrance to the house, a swimming pool, or any other area that will attract a high level of traffic. A primary path should be a minimum of 4 feet wide, which is enough room for two people to walk comfortably side by side. Because people generally pay less attention to where they're stepping when traveling a path they use on a regular basis, choose materials that will remain flat and even to avoid a tripping hazard. Concrete, mortared flagstone, or tightly laid bricks or pavers are all good choices. Stepping-stone pathways that have wide spaces between them filled with sand or gravel are not recommended, as they will wear unevenly, particularly in climates with significant rainfall.

Secondary paths that meander through the garden and are used less frequently do not need excessive width. Natural materials provide attractive contrast to surrounding greenery.

Secondary pathways are those that lead to lesser-used elements like side benches or fire pits, or meander through planting beds. Because these pathways don't see as much foot traffic, a narrower width of 2.5 to 3 feet is usually adequate. The exception is secondary pathways that will be used to move equipment around for day-to-day garden chores, such as lawnmowers or wheelbarrows. In these instances, ensure the path is at least 3 feet wide and is paved with a material that easily accommodates sturdy, wheeled equipment.

Incorporating a pathway in an ultra-restricted space like a side yard can be tricky, as there is a natural assumption that the path should be especially narrow to avoid overwhelming the space. Surprisingly, the opposite is true. Making a path too narrow can unintentionally create the impression of a child-sized space, which in turn will make the whole area feel smaller.

Beyond being practical, pathways can add significantly to the charm and attractiveness of a backyard. It's important to understand that movement and circulation can have very different functions when you are outside versus inside. Indoors, the

Saltillo tiles contrast with landings paved with gold fines, making steps highly visible and easy to navigate.

purpose of hallways, stairs, and other open areas is to get quickly and easily from Point A to Point B. The opposite is true in a garden, where the experience of getting from one area to another can be as important as the final destination. Faster and more direct isn't necessarily better; paths that meander remind you to stop and smell flowers or admire a specimen tree from a different vantage point. Avoid pathways that are a straight shot. Instead, incorporate gentle curves or add an angular jog to a straight path to subtly encourage travelers to slow down and enjoy the garden. Remember that the garden's visitors include *you* — investing time to transform simple garden elements into interactive experiences turns your backyard into an irresistible destination.

Outdoor stairs have their own set of rules, too, distinct from an indoor staircase. In fact, there is a specific formula for determining optimum stairway dimensions so people can move up and down in a comfortable and predictable way. The height of the rise (the vertical height of the step, R) and the tread (the horizontal width of the step, T) should be 2R + T = 24 to 27 inches. Indoors, it is common to pair a 6-inch riser with a 12-inch tread; plugged into the formula, this would equate to 2(6 inches) + 12 inches = 24 inches. While this technically falls within the desired range, in a backyard, one of the goals is to foster a sense that the movement is slower and more contemplative, or just *different* than movement indoors. Smaller treads with steeper risers have a cramped, utilitarian feel, making them less comfortable to walk on. People using them subconsciously want to hurry up. These treads also physically accommodate less of a walker's sole, which means the user must pay close attention and look down at the steps instead of looking around the garden.

The ideal range for garden treads is 14 to 16 inches. This is wide enough to create a gracious effect and encourage a slower pace, but not so wide that it interrupts someone's normal stride. My personal favorite is a 5.5-inch rise and a 15-inch tread.

Because of the tendency to pay less attention to stairs outside, it is important to keep stairways safe. You must put some kind of visual indicator on the edge of each step, to avoid creating a tripping hazard. This can be done by adding a finish that extends over the stair, such as a bullnose finish (which creates a shadow and a change in pattern), by including a border in a different color or material, or even by adding a border of the same material but in a different pattern. This is especially important if you have only one step, as it can be particularly easy to overlook or gauge. Apart from safety, embellishing a staircase in a thoughtful or unexpected way transforms it into a memorable and unique garden feature, rather than just a utilitarian element.

Double-Duty Design

A successful garden is built foremost on a foundation of solid design principles, but I admit to a secret fondness for furniture, products, and gadgets that do more than one thing, whether that's a jar of coconut oil that conditions your hair and flavors your popcorn, or a footstool that serves as additional seating when needed. Outdoors, including built elements, furnishings, or even plants that do double duty is an excellent way to squeeze every bit of enjoyment out of small spaces.

Raised beds flanked by stairs add an attractive level change to the garden, as well as spaces to perch.

A stucco retaining wall capped with 8-inch-wide bullnose bricks does double duty by providing extra garden seating.

Entertaining space

Understanding how a backyard will truly be used helps create a garden that is both beautiful and functional. An important part of space planning is determining how many people a garden needs to accommodate. For day-to-day use, this is simple. Just count the number of members in your family, and you're done. But what about when company comes? Once you've created your backyard oasis, you'll want to ensure there is enough space to entertain friends and extended family. It isn't always practical or even aesthetically pleasing to create a large dining or conversation area that is meant to hold eight or ten guests when usually it's just you and your spouse. So how do you create flexible space?

That's where double-duty design comes in. By incorporating clever hardscape elements and accessories in advance that can act as temporary seating areas or dining spots, it is possible to create a garden that is the right size for everyday living, but can also accommodate larger groups on special occasions.

Seat walls

One of the most attractive and practical ways to add flexible seating is via retaining walls. These are often added to gardens that are sloped or very hilly to hold back soil, but they also create more level living space. By adding structure to patios or planted areas, retaining walls also help define and delineate areas of the garden. Beyond that, if thoughtfully constructed, they can do double duty as seating.

There are two critical elements to a successful seat wall: height and material. The most comfortable height for a seat wall is 18 inches, which is the typical height

of a dining or other indoor chair. If you can, situate your seat wall in an area of the garden where the soil of a slope can be carved as close to that height as possible. Soil can be moved around fairly easily, which means if there's a slope to your yard at all, it's probably possible to build up the soil to the desired height. Alternatively, a tiered series of walls can be incorporated if the slope is very steep.

Material choice is also crucial. Materials that work well are not only sturdy and durable enough to retain soil without bowing or sagging, but are also wide enough at the top for comfortable seating. This width can be from 6 to 12 inches. Not all materials commonly used to build retaining walls will work well if the goal is also to provide seating. Because their surface is uneven and cannot be capped, dry-stacked stone walls do not easily double as seating options. If the construction of the fence is very basic, wood is also not an optimal choice. While wood retaining walls are inexpensive, because of the way they are constructed, their posts are necessarily exposed, giving the impression that the back of the wall is facing forward. This can be addressed by facing the front of the wall with decorative wooden planks, thereby

Concrete is an excellent material choice for gardens designed in a contemporary style.

hiding the posts. You can also employ wood fences in areas that are less visible, where they can be camouflaged with either trailing plants spilling over the top or mounding plants planted in front. (However, this makes them impractical to sit on.)

Your material choice should be guided by whatever hardscapes are already part of the backyard, as well as your garden's overall style. For a contemporary look, poured-in-place concrete makes an elegant, modern statement. A wall like this can be molded into almost any shape—straight or curved. A range of colors can be added to concrete, and it is easily customized for different heights, widths, and thicknesses, creating a finished look that is sleek and contemporary.

Another common material for building retaining walls is cinderblock. When stacked and mortared, the individual bricks create a durable wall that can be faced with a variety of materials and finished with a decorative cap. A stucco finish is a popular choice for Mediterranean-style homes and also an excellent option to tie the landscape to the residence if your home's exterior is faced with stucco. A stucco finish also allows for decorative accents such as tiles to be incorporated into the wall's facade.

Completing a cinderblock wall with a stone veneer is another attractive option that complements a wide range of design styles, from traditional to rustic. Cost and construction options vary. The most affordable veneers are panels constructed with man-made materials like polyurethane that are designed to mimic the look of natural stone or brick. Cultured stone panels in a stacked or random pattern are an excellent choice for a veneer that is relatively easy to attach, and they can look and feel virtually identical to quarried or field stone. Walls can also be faced with natural materials such as brick, stone, or tile, although these are generally more expensive.

While the wall itself may be narrow, the wall cap should be wide enough to comfortably perch on. The minimum recommended width is 6 inches, but for a typical 6-inch-wide wall, an 8- to 10-inch cap is preferable. Not only is a wider seat more comfortable, but having a cap that overlaps by an inch or two is an attractive way to finish a wall. I often top stucco walls with 8-inch bull-nosed bricks in a darker, coordinating color. The smooth, neutral-colored finish of concrete tiles is another attractive choice to balance the multi-hued, textural look of stone walls.

If you want to enjoy the presence and practicality a seat wall provides but your backyard is flat, just adopt the concept by creating a garden wall. The difference between the two types of wall is simply that a garden wall is installed for purely aesthetic reasons. Since it is not actually holding back soil, it is generally less expensive to construct and does not need to be as thick or sturdy, but otherwise follows the same design principles as a retaining wall.

Raised beds built from decorative materials are both functional and attractive.

Raised beds

Often viewed as purely utilitarian, vegetable beds tend to be relegated to side yards or the outer reaches of a garden. They don't need to be banished or hidden from sight, however. The key is to make them both functional and attractive by

following the same principles used when designing a garden wall. A common height for most raised beds is 12 inches, but by increasing the height to 18 inches and adding a ledge or cap that is about 6 inches wide, not only will you create additional seating space, but typical chores like weeding and harvesting will be much more comfortable since you can sit on the edge of the box rather than having to kneel on the ground. Also—guests love to see what is growing! Why not make it simple for them by making beds easy to reach and comfortable to sit on?

This is a place where inexpensive wood can shine. Wood beds that are unfinished will weather to a dull gray, so consider staining them to create a look more akin to built-in furniture. The finish that a coat of stain or paint provides will tie raised beds into the rest of the garden as well.

If your backyard is small or oddly shaped, remember there's no reason vegetable boxes must be the standard 4-by-6-foot rectangle. Beds that are long and narrow may fit more easily into tighter spaces, and small squares can be a better choice for defining space in modest gardens. If you are fortunate enough to have a large yard, keep in mind that a series of smaller beds can be a more effective visual choice than one or two massive ones. Not only can excessively large beds overwhelm the space, it is also difficult to plant or harvest from a raised bed that is more than 4 feet wide. If the bed can only be accessed from one side, limit the width to between 2 and 3 feet.

Blurring the lines

Additional seating can also be added in sneakier ways. In fact, when not in use, some seating might not look anything at all like a chair or bench. Landscape rock nestled in a garden is a charming way to add a textural contrast to plants, and is particularly effective in the context of a more natural or rustic-looking design. When placing decorative rock close to a patio or play area, include at least one stone feature that is large and flat enough to serve as a seat. Lower and more interesting than a standard chair, seat rocks are particularly attractive to children, so consider positioning one near a play area. Situating a seat rock close to a small pond or water feature invites kids and grown-ups alike to get close and enjoy the sight and sound of moving water.

If your garden includes steps, expect that at some point someone will use them as seating. To encourage people to sit on

Oversized landscape rock can also work as a place to sit.

This clever piece of garden art makes a perfect child-sized seat.

them, consider making the tread 18 inches deep; this works best if you only have a few steps since this is wider than is comfortable for a walking cadence. A larger stair like this adds a gracious note to a garden, while also creating enough space both for seating and for guests to set down glasses or plates.

Artwork and accessories you choose for the garden can create seating opportunities as well. Look for carved wooden pieces or ceramic statuary with flat areas that can double as footstools, small benches, or side tables.

Combine seating with storage

The glossy pages of home and garden magazines provide great inspiration, but editorial styling can also lead to unrealistic expectations. The perfection we see in print is almost always impossible to maintain in a typical backyard, where family members, pets, and seasonal plant changes mean a certain level of clutter or debris is inevitable. If you spend time outside on a regular basis, your garden will attract the clutter of everyday life, the same way your kitchen table is scattered with sunglasses, coffee cups, and yesterday's mail. Be realistic and include outdoor storage in your design, whether as a place for furniture cushions, gardening tools, or kids' toys. Instead of unsightly plastic bins, opt for attractively finished storage chests that can double as benches. If you invest in quality storage pieces, you'll be more likely to keep them in sight – this in turn keeps the items you need in a handy place that you won't be ashamed to use as additional patio seating. Storage benches are available at home improvement stores and online in a range of sizes, colors, and styles.

Planting strategies

Double-duty design strategies apply to plant choices as well as hardscape and furnishings. While garden centers are adept at creating enticing displays that highlight exotic flowers or richly colored blossoms, before indulging in a major impulse purchase, take time to consider how appealing those new plants will be a few weeks later when the last of the flowers are spent. By seeking out plants that offer more than one benefit or put on a show in multiple seasons, your garden will continue to be interesting long after your neighbor's petunias have been relegated to the compost heap.

Homegrown fruits and vegetables are on many homeowners' lists of must-haves. One of the most popular ways to grow produce is in raised beds, but not every backyard has enough space for them. Even when space is available, raised beds are not a style fit for every garden, particularly when a refined look is desired. Fortunately, there are plenty of edibles with foliage and flowers attractive enough to double as ornamentals, making them as easy to mix into the landscape as a traditional shrub or perennial.

Edible plants such as blueberries are handsome enough to be ornamental as well.

edible and ornamental

Typically, vegetables and other edible plants are segregated from the rest of the garden or confined to raised beds along the perimeter of the yard. For smaller spaces that lack room for a traditional kitchen garden, choose edible varieties whose good looks make them right at home planted among the prettiest of ornamental plants.

Plant	USDA zones	Description
'Imperial Star' artichoke (*Cynara scolymus* 'Imperial Star')	9 (annual in other zones)	With their dramatic, silvery green leaves, and stunning summer flowers, artichokes make an elegant addition to an ornamental garden. 'Imperial Star' is an improved cultivar that bears fruit in its first year and boasts less prickly stems than older varieties.
'Bull's Blood' beet (*Beta vulgaris* 'Bull's Blood')	Annual in all zones	The burgundy leaves of this mild-flavored beet make an arresting foil to nearby plants with silver or chartreuse foliage. When picked young, the leaves are tender enough to be mixed into salads. A great choice for semi-shady gardens.
pineapple guava (*Feijoa sellowiana*)	9–10	An excellent evergreen anchor for hot, dry gardens. Two-toned leaves set off red and white flowers that cover the tree in spring. The taste of the small, oblong fruits has been described as a cross between pineapple and Juicy Fruit chewing gum.
'Sunshine Blue' blueberry (*Vaccinium* 'Sunshine Blue')	5–9	This sun-loving shrub marks the beginning of spring with delicate, soft-pink blooms, followed in midsummer with a crop of juicy berries. More productive when planted in multiples, so consider massing several together.
sweet bay (*Laurus nobilis*)	5–9	Dark green, highly aromatic leaves should be dried before adding to recipes; fresh leaves have a bitter taste. Wait a few years to begin harvesting leaves—they become more flavorful as they mature.
'Lapins' cherry tree (*Prunus avium* 'Lapins')	5–9	Cherries taste similar to 'Bing', but are larger and more split-resistant. Good for small spaces, as 'Lapins' is self-pollinating, meaning two trees are not required for it to produce fruit. Stunning white blossoms in spring; vibrant, hot-colored foliage in summer.

clockwise, from top left
'Imperial Star' artichoke, 'Bull's Blood' beet, 'Sunshine Blue' blueberry, 'Lapins' cherry tree, sweet bay, pine-apple guava

double-duty herbs

It's the rare homeowner that doesn't make room for at least a few herbs. While planting herbs in containers is hardly a new idea, consider moving beyond the old standbys that make for a monotonous bowl of green, green, and green, and instead look for less common versions of the classics. Not only will this ratchet up the flavor at summer barbecues, but by choosing herbs in a mix of colors and textures—not to mention sneaking in a few non-edible flowering herbs—you'll have a piece of living garden art that's as eye-catching as it is practical.

Keep an herb container garden simple by favoring perennial herbs over annual varieties to avoid having to replant every year. Many perennial herbs, including the ones listed here, require less water than annual herbs once they've had a year to establish—a bonus if you occasionally forget to water. These six versatile herbs from the mint family are also superstars on the grill.

Herb	USDA Zones	Description
Cuban oregano (*Plectranthus amboinicus*)	5–9	With a heartier flavor profile than Italian oregano and a hint of lemon when leaves are crushed, Cuban oregano is a popular choice for highly spiced Indian and Filipino cuisine.
CHEF'S CHOICE rosemary (*Rosemary officinalis* 'Roman Beauty' PP18192)	7–9	The name says it all. Who wouldn't want a rosemary preferred by chefs? Choose this variety for its higher oil content, spicy flavor, and compact habit that responds well to container culture.
'Tricolor' sage (*Salvia officinalis* 'Tricolor')	6–9	The mix of burgundy, cream, and green on the leaves of tricolor sage provide soft contrast to other container herbs, while its traditional flavor means it can be subbed for any recipe that calls for ordinary garden sage.
'Highland Cream' thyme (*Thymus praecox* 'Highland Cream')	5–9	With its creamy, two-toned leaves and mounding habit, 'Highland Cream' makes an attractive ornamental and culinary herb. Thyme is a natural complement to potatoes, peppers, and roasted root vegetables.

Herb	USDA Zones	Description
'Pesto Perpetuo' basil (*Ocimum ×citriodorum* 'Pesto Perpetuo')	9–11 (annual in all zones)	The featured ingredient of homemade pesto. Its variegated leaves make an outstanding garnish and add contrast to a container of mixed herbs. Its real star power, however, is in its longevity. 'Pesto Perpetuo' doesn't flower, so leaves retain their flavor indefinitely.
'Kent Beauty' oregano (*Origanum* 'Kent Beauty')	6–10	Although it has no culinary value, adding a purely ornamental herb such as 'Kent Beauty' oregano to your herb mix means your composition will be beautiful and functional. Blended foliage in shades of blue-green, chartreuse, and pale pink holds its color over a long season.

clockwise, from top left
Cuban oregano, CHEF'S CHOICE rosemary, 'Pesto Perpetuo' basil, 'Kent Beauty' oregano, 'Tricolor' sage, 'Highland Cream' thyme

above Witch alder in summer (left) and fall (right).

opposite 'Orange Dream' Japanese maple in spring (top) and summer (bottom).

Multi-season superstars

Choosing evergreen plants that feature foliage in a consistent range of colors and textures, and making them the backbone of your plan, is a classic way to design a garden with year-round beauty that doesn't demand excessive maintenance. While this creates a sturdy foundation, elevate your garden to the next level by rounding out your palette with plants that highlight seasonal changes. Plants' ability to mark the passage of time—whether through a sunny display of spring flowers, a blaze of autumn color, or brightly hued berries in the winter—is an important component to crafting a garden with a unique character. And there's no need to rely strictly on plants that add only one season of drama—there are many selections that put on one show in the spring and an entirely different display later in the year.

Witch alder (*Fothergilla* 'Mount Airy'), a medium-sized shrub that thrives in colder parts of the country, welcomes spring with a profusion of lightly scented, fluffy white blooms. Metallic green foliage makes it an excellent shrub for contrast with other acid-loving favorites like rhododendrons and camellias. Autumn is when the real drama takes place, though, when witch alder ignites into a blaze of fiery orange-red, providing brilliant contrast to evergreen shrubs nearby. Hardy to USDA zones 5–9.

Spring flowers chased by fall color is the most common way for a plant to offer double-duty service, but some plants' foliage display alone is so varied and colorful, flowers aren't missed. In spring, 'Orange Dream' Japanese maple (*Acer palmatum* 'Orange Dream') unfurls chartreuse leaves banded with pink margins. By summer, leaves have turned a soft shade of pale green. Autumn introduces the most dramatic color change, as the foliage transforms a final time into a rich shade of burnt orange. This small tree rarely grows above 12 feet and is hardy to USDA zones 5–9.

While the vivid colors of changing leaves are hallmarks of autumn, plants that offer more subtle seasonal beauty are also worthy of consideration. Sweet autumn clematis (*Clematis paniculata*) is a classic cottage garden plant boasting pure white, sweetly scented flowers in summer. What sets this plant apart from other climbing vines is its autumn appearance, when the flowers are replaced by masses of delicate, silvery seed heads. Left unchecked, sweet autumn clematis can reach a height of 30 feet, but small-space gardeners will have no problem keeping growth in check with a hard pruning in spring. Hardy to USDA zones 4–9.

For cold-weather gardeners, winter is often the dreariest time in the garden, as snow blanketing the ground turns most shrubs into indistinct lumps. The solution is structural plants that retain their architectural shape even when laden with snow. With its intricate, twisted form, Harry Lauder's walking stick (*Corylus avellana* 'Contorta') fits the bill perfectly. In late winter, pale yellow catkins droop from bare limbs. In summer, its branches are covered with dense green or red foliage, but early winter is when the best show starts. Stripped of its leaves, this small tree makes an unusual winter specimen as its smooth branches contort themselves into elegantly twisted shapes. It can be pruned to a compact shape to make a 12- to 20-foot tree in the garden. Hardy to USDA zones 4–9.

above Harry Lauder's walking stick in summer (left) and winter (right).

opposite Sweet autumn clematis in summer (top) and fall (bottom).

small garden, big impact

Exploring a smaller backyard is akin to peeling back the layers of an onion. The first layer is the most immediate: What do you see when you first step outside? Design strategies that extend a garden's footprint — either literally (by planting in unexpected places) or imaginatively (by crafting the illusion of more space) — help sidestep the unwelcome sensation that with one quick look around, you've seen all there is to see.

Sight is the most direct way to engage with a garden, but it is not the only way outdoor spaces pull us in. In a thoughtfully planned garden, our initial assessment of it only stokes our enthusiasm to delve deeper — it should hint at nooks to be explored and pleasures to be uncovered. This is where the intimate scale of a small backyard becomes a real asset. By incorporating details that add layers of visual intrigue, you can create a uniquely intense, interactive garden experience that isn't easily replicated in large backyards or broader landscapes.

The addition of level changes, colorful plants, containers, and accessories adds layers of interest to a small space.

Finding Space

One key to expanding any garden's perceived size is to utilize nontraditional spaces. So while the logical place to begin a new backyard design is with an accurate measurement that clearly represents its total area, it's equally important to remember that a backyard can be much more than just the ground immediately underfoot. Likewise, to add additional impact to an existing space – one with patios and planting beds that won't be changing, or can't – you must look beyond the ground plane.

One of the most popular and enduring trends in recent years has been vertical gardening, for the straightforward reason that turning walls, fences, and other upright structures into growing surfaces is a clever way to add more plants to tight spaces. Growing plants on walls is often employed as a utilitarian solution, for example by vegetable gardeners in search of ways to grow more edible crops. But going vertical also provides ornamental gardeners with a fantastic opportunity to make an impact. Instead of leaving fences bare or smothering them with unruly vines, consider turning some of these surfaces into focal-point walls.

When we enter a space, our eyes have a natural tendency to follow the strongest lines. In a garden where large expanses of wall or fence are left exposed, these become the dominant lines of the garden by default, naturally drawing the gaze of visitors even if these elements have long since become invisible to owners. It is hard to imagine a less impactful, inadvertent focal point than a plain wood fence. To remedy this, consider a design strategy more commonly associated with interior design and treat your fence like a blank wall that would benefit from embellishment or accessories.

Your approach to how simple or complex to make a perimeter wall's decoration should depend in part on the furnishings and plants close to the wall. For surfaces located behind planting beds, particularly if some of those plants are tall enough to obscure part of the wall, simply adding a wash of paint may be enough to transform it from mundane to remarkable. Choose bold colors to make a dramatic statement, or softer tones for a subtler impact. Providing your plants with a colorful backdrop also integrates vertical and horizontal elements, turning what may have been a simple grouping of plants into a true vignette.

Adding art to plain surfaces, particularly a fence or wall adjacent to a planned seating area, is another effective way to take advantage of the space you have. Keep in mind that because a garden is alive, the exuberance of even a lightly planted garden necessarily means a certain level of visual chaos. Because of this, consider limiting wall décor to a single, bold item such as a planted living wall, a mirror, or an outdoor wall sculpture. Mimicking the type of focal points used with interior design in an outdoor space also helps reinforce to visitors that a patio's seating area is a distinct destination – which in turn creates another type of space on which the eye can rest. The placement of other outdoor décor items can further reinforce this if they are grouped to highlight the wall's accent piece.

A vivid blue garden wall provides attractive contrast to surrounding plants.

Creating the Illusion of Space

In many ways, small gardens are a boon, as it is possible to create more atmosphere with much less effort. Still, there's no question that they can feel confining. Fortunately, the yardstick that measures a successful garden is less about the perfection of its individual components, and more about how we respond to the space as a whole. That's where illusion comes in. Incorporating a few simple techniques that give the impression your garden is bigger than it really is will combat that too-small feeling.

Well incorporated, mirrors can be a simple but effective tool for expanding a garden's perceived boundaries. There's a reason a mirror over the fireplace mantel is such a popular design choice in living rooms – reflecting back a portion of the room is an easy way to add spaciousness and elegance to an enclosed area. A mirror hung on an outdoor wall or fence performs a similar function. When positioned near a seating area, it helps give the space a finished appearance, and by reflecting back the details of the garden, it creates the illusion that the space is larger than it actually is.

Incorporating mirrors in more adventurous ways can add a truly magical element to a garden. Since a mirror hung outdoors is not expected, it's often not instantly recognized as such. Nestled among the foliage, reflecting back the greenery of the garden, it feels like a viewport to another realm. To maximize the impact of unconventionally placed mirrors, play around with locations. High on a fence, a small mirror masquerades as a window to a different part of the garden. Leaned against a wall lower down, it creates the impression of a child-sized door to a secret garden, particularly if a few artfully placed stepping-stones lead up to it. For maximum effect, place mirrors in heavily planted areas. Partially obscuring a mirror with plants and outdoor décor makes it that much harder to identify, adding to the likelihood that people will walk over to it to investigate. It is important to be aware of what the mirror faces – branches, leaves, and flowers are what you want the mirror to reflect. Hanging one opposite a blank wall or open stretch of garden will destroy the fantasy. If the place you want to hang a mirror doesn't have the best reflected view, you can always try tilting it toward a greener part of the garden.

Any strategy that leaves the impression there is more garden to explore will add to the illusion of extra space. While the tendency may be to focus all your design energy on the primary living spaces in the backyard, remember that you don't have to relegate a side yard to becoming a utilitarian storage area or uninspiring pass-through. Even when it is impractical to fully landscape your home's side yards, using even a portion of them to visually extend a garden's area will avoid making it look like your garden ends abruptly at the edges of the house. Stopping the backyard's interesting areas flush with the sides of the house creates an unbroken line, reinforcing the long, narrow profile the overall layout should be trying to minimize. Even when the design focus is primarily on the main backyard, you can incorporate what I've dubbed "disappearing pathways." Extending a path and its surrounding plantings just a few feet around the corner creates the illusion of spaciousness and

One carefully sited piece of living wall art is enough to turn a simple fence into a focal point wall.

mirror placement

Mirrors don't always need to be eye level.

There are a few practical considerations when placing mirrors in the garden. Shady areas, where bright sunlight won't be reflected back, are ideal. Not only will placement in these darker locations keep annoying or even hazardous flashes of light from reflecting back into the garden, but a shadier spot will also minimize the possibility that the mirror is in the flight path of birds.

leads the viewer to believe there's more garden to see. The fact that the pathway may lead to nothing more exciting than trash receptacles or the compost bin can stay your little secret.

Walls are a time-honored method for adding structure to a garden, but in small backyards, using plants to create separation between spaces accomplishes the same goal, without overwhelming the yard or blocking it off visually from borrowed views or other areas of the garden. Sheared, dense shrubs can also have the undesired effect of making a garden seem as if it's been separated into small, disconnected spaces, inadvertently creating a cramped feeling – the opposite of what you want to achieve when adding greenery. To make a small yard feel luxuriously private without crowding, consider what are dubbed see-through plants. Tall and airy plants create a permeable border that subtly separates one area from the next, as the gaps between their branches or leaves allow glimpses of the garden beyond. Grasses are an obvious choice for this, but many perennials and annuals provide a similar effect. Look for plants with an open framework of stems, as opposed to mounding plants with an abundance of leaves or flowers.

For the most part, herbaceous plants – those with soft stems, such as most perennials – work best to create a see-through effect, as woodier shrubs tend to be tightly formed. Plants that are less densely leafed and can be pruned into an open, attractive shape are the exception. Moderately sized manzanitas (*Arctostaphylos densiflora*) such as 'Howard McMinn' or 'Sentinel' are good examples. With attractive cinnamon-colored bark and naturally sculptural forms, both of these cultivars can be trained into small, open tree shapes to create a tall, permeable border.

Avoid placing mirrors too high, and stick to shadier spots where birds are unlikely to encounter them.

top left Paths that weave through the garden signal visitors that there is more garden to explore.

bottom See-through plants like tall verbena (*Verbena bonariensis*) act as permeable garden walls.

top right Don't stop patios or pathways flush with the edge of the house. Continuing hardscape around the corner of the house—even a few feet—creates the illusion of a larger space.

see-through plants

Even small gardens benefit from structural elements that help define spaces, but incorporating them without overpowering the landscape can be tricky. Because of their open, loosely branching habit, see-through plants create the illusion of separation, while still allowing views into other parts of the garden.

Plant	USDA zones	Description
burnet (*Sanguisorba menziesii*)	4–9	Slender stems and narrow-profile blooms create an attractive see-through effect. Dark maroon flowers that resemble pussy willow catkins top feathery, blue-gray foliage. 18 inches wide by 2.5 feet tall.
'Blonde Ambition' grama grass (*Bouteloua gracilis* 'Blonde Ambition')	4–9	A hardy ornamental grass, 2.5 to 3 feet wide and tall, with striking blue-green foliage. Medium-sized spikes of wheat-colored stalks topped by unusual, flag-shaped flowers in summer.
dwarf lion's tail (*Leonotis menthifolia*)	9–10	An evergreen shrub whose structure resembles that of a perennial. Tubular whorls of fuzzy, orange flowers on tall stems add both architectural interest and color. 4 to 5 feet wide and tall.
pink vervain (*Verbena hastata* 'Rosea')	3–9	Delicate arching flowers grow in cup-shaped whorls on stalks, resembling an elegant candelabrum. Notable for dark pinkish purple buds that open to a rich rose color. 2 feet wide and 3 to 4 feet tall.
kangaroo paw (*Anigozanthos* spp.)	9–11	Flowers rise on slender stalks 2 to 4 feet above a base of strappy green leaves. Seek out selections from the Velvet series, whose leaves are less susceptible to turning black in cold weather. 2 to 6 feet high and 18 inches to 3 feet wide.
torch lily (*Kniphofia uvaria*)	5–9	Stately, narrow flower stalks rise above slender, bright green leaves. Stems grow from 2 to 5 feet depending on variety, so check labels. Heat, cold and drought tolerant. 2 to 5 feet high and 1 to 3 feet wide.

clockwise, from top left
dwarf lion's tail, burnet, 'Blonde Ambition' grama grass, pink vervain, kangaroo paw, torch lily

A Sense of Discovery

By its very nature, a small garden has a correspondingly intimate scale. This means visitors will be able to see most of it up close as they move through it. Consider this an advantage: it presents the opportunity to include details that make the garden truly welcoming and unique. One of the simplest and most enjoyable ways to add a sense of discovery and to encourage thoughtful and leisurely strolls through a small garden is to tuck in a few surprises. This can be as simple as rethinking placement of ordinary garden elements, like containers and garden art.

Rather than limiting containers to traditional locations like patios and stairs, consider scattering them throughout the landscape. When set unexpectedly into the back or middle of a planted bed where they aren't immediately on display from the most-trafficked areas, they invite closer inspection. Including structural elements like containers in untraditional spaces like planting beds also provides welcome contrasts in texture and pleasantly confounds our expectations.

From a practical standpoint, containers can also be problem solvers for parts of the garden where planting is challenging. A good example of this might be under mature trees whose established root systems leave little space for new plants, or trees whose physiology makes them inhospitable to other plants. Trees like this are referred to as allelopathic, which means their roots secrete biochemicals that interfere with a nearby plant's ability to thrive. Common examples include black walnut (*Juglans nigra*), sycamore (*Platanus* spp.), and eucalyptus. Because it is generally a chore to hand water the outer perimeter of the backyard, avoid high-maintenance plant choices for containers and opt for low-water shrubs and perennials that can thrive with a minimum of attention. In warm climates, for example, succulents are an excellent choice.

Containers aren't just for patios and porches. Mix them into the landscape for more layers of visual interest.

right A tiny sports figure tucked in a planting bed is a whimsical way to show support for your favorite team.

opposite Requiring minimal care, succulents make a good choice for containers located away from a ready source of water.

Besides mixing containers into the landscape, why not tuck surprises into the containers themselves? Half-hidden by leafy greenery, what could be more fun than discovering an unexpected garden fairy or pint-sized gnome peeking up at you? Surprises like this don't need to be traditional outdoor décor purchased at the garden center. Tuck in toys or figurines—have a sense of humor about it. Or choose small items that reflect your personal hobbies. Personalization adds a whimsical, memorable touch to a garden.

Diagonal Design

Garden designs that rely on diagonal lines have a particularly bold impact in narrow backyards and side yards, because they effectively combat the bowling-alley effect. Unlike traditional geometric designs, where layouts are usually parallel or perpendicular to the house, this approach tilts axis lines on an angle to make a garden feel spacious in multiple ways. Just as the hypotenuse is the longest line in a right triangle, arranging the dominant line of the garden between opposite corners rather than from side to side aligns the garden with the two points that are farthest apart. By interrupting the strong rectangular shapes created by the lines of the house and the backyard's boundaries, a diagonal axis helps our eyes skip from focal point to focal point within. This effect

hide and seek

Young guests have come to love the hiding starfish in my garden.

While visiting a craft fair, I purchased three inexpensive ceramic starfish from a local artisan. Although I initially placed them carefully throughout the garden to highlight pathways and flowering perennials, over the years, the starfish have taken on a life of their own, traveling around the backyard seemingly at will. One of my favorite ways to enjoy their refusal to stay in one place is to make a game of it. When young children visit me, I'll send them out into the garden to hunt for the starfish. Once they've been successfully located, I invite my guests to place the sea creatures in new hiding places—for the next visitor to discover.

can be amplified by varying the width of any patios or pathways along that line in a staggered pattern, so that planting pockets and hardscape intermingle. Ensuring that hardscape is nestled into lush plants also keeps activity areas inviting, while the plants' free-form shapes are crucial to breaking up the line of sight. This in turn brings an air of mystery and a sense that more of the garden is yet to be uncovered. On a practical note, this design strategy also helps create activity areas with ample space in proportion to the overall area of the yard.

Diagonal design does not have to be an all-or-nothing proposition. Although it is an exciting way to organize a small garden or side yard overall, its principles can also be used to soften any strongly rectangular space in an existing garden. Laying square-shaped pavers, tiles, or flagstones on the diagonal will help counterbalance a rigid, rectangular patio. Even a simple gesture like orienting an outdoor area rug or furniture at an angle is enough to soften rectangular spaces.

Creating pathways that zigzag indirectly through the garden is a time-honored and excellent way to encourage visitors to slow down and enjoy the space, but one word of caution: don't go overboard with directional changes on any path that is used for primary circulation. Forcing walkers to shift direction repeatedly when they really just need to get from Point A to Point B quickly becomes an annoyance. If people are forced to go too far out of their way on a daily basis, the unintended (but likely) result will be that they tramp a shortcut through your carefully planned garden beds.

Arranging the seating area on the diagonal helps break up the boxiness of this small suburban courtyard.

opposite Organizing a garden on the diagonal is an excellent strategy for energizing a narrow space.

Lawn or No Lawn?

Of all the things we can grow in our backyards, a lush, green lawn is probably the single most popular element, so ingrained in our sense of what makes a backyard respectable-looking that it transcends regionality and even practicality. For over 75 years, a backyard with a huge swath of lawn has been an integral part of the iconic American suburban lifestyle. When I began my career as a garden designer fifteen years ago, it was the rare client who didn't request the inclusion of at least a modest-sized lawn in a backyard landscape design. Lately, the question of whether a garden plan should include a lawn at all comes up a lot more often.

The expectation that lawn should be an automatic component of a backyard is beginning to change. Recurring droughts in the Southeast and West have made homeowners much more selective as to where scarce water resources should be spent. Concerns for the impact on watershed health in the Northeast have also led communities to question the wisdom of using standard lawn-care chemicals. In the Midwest, a rediscovered appreciation of the biodiversity that occurs in native meadows has

Adapted native species that require less maintenance and water can still be pet friendly.

right This small-size lawn is appropriately scaled to the patio and surrounding garden.

resulted in a shift in the definition of what a lawn can be. All these examples point to a growing national awareness that lawns—at least those grown from non-native species that require supplemental water and chemicals to sustain—are not always the best choice.

When your lot is modestly sized, a thoughtful approach to how much turf (if any) to include should be part of your planning process. If the goal is a design that maximizes impact, lawns by their very nature work against this effect. Traditional sod lawns eat up a disproportionate amount of real estate, crowding out the living spaces, structures, and ornamental spaces that bring a small garden to life.

That said, there are good reasons to keep some space devoted to lawn. Although there are other ground covers that can handle foot traffic, it is hard to beat traditional, regularly maintained sod for many outdoor activities. If you have young children, including a patch of turf for play can be a smart lifestyle choice. Likewise, those with dogs often want a place for their pets to exercise. Even so, before you opt for lawn, take time to think through how much you really need. In modest yards, lawns may be too small to be practical. If there isn't a stretch big enough for throw-

ing a Frisbee or playing a game of tag, you might be better served using the neighborhood park for such activities and devoting the backyard to different kinds of creative play besides sports, such as a sandbox, playhouse, or play structure.

There are, however, a number of compelling reasons to consider eliminating—or at least downsizing—a backyard lawn. First among these is a desire to spend more time enjoying a garden and less time maintaining it. Ditching the weekly drudgery of lawn care is one of the easiest ways to make this happen. While trimming or weeding can be ignored for long stretches with no real damage done, skipping the tasks associated with regular lawn maintenance isn't an option. If a lawn is just being used as something pretty to look at, do you really need one at all? After all, that's real estate that could be used for growing vegetables, fitting in a quiet spot to read or relax, or adding more entertainment space. In general, lawns add an aesthetic quality that's perceived as nice to an average-sized backyard, but that's about it.

Design solutions for replacing lawn

One of the challenges of limiting or eliminating lawn in a backyard is figuring out exactly what to do with that space instead. If you know you want more patio space to accommodate additional seating or garden features, then it's a straightforward transaction of swapping lawn for hardscape. But if the goal is to create a more attractive and interactive aesthetic, suddenly all that newly liberated space can feel daunting.

As much as I applaud downsizing lawns for cultural and lifestyle reasons, from a design standpoint, a lawn does make it easier to come up with a pleasing layout. A large swath of lawn creates negative space, which acts as a resting place for the eye that keeps the overall design easy to read. In a traditional backyard, the lawn typically occupies center stage next to the patio, with planted areas and other garden elements orbiting around its edges. Because of this, it becomes the neutral connection that unites these different garden elements. If you exclude lawn in the new design, it is important to introduce a new unifier.

One solution is to borrow the concept of a stroll garden. Popular on English country estates in the 1800s, this design style is characterized by meandering gravel walks leading through an open park. Trees and shrubbery were planted in groupings to mimic nature—replacing the hedgerows, parterres, and straight lines that had been popular until then—while whimsical small structures and statues were placed artfully throughout to create stopping points of interest and contemplation. The goal was to blend the house into the surrounding countryside and to create a more enjoyable, relaxed way to interact with the outdoors than was possible with the more formal garden styles of preceding generations.

Fortunately, you don't need a large estate to create your own version of a stroll garden. Introducing a series of winding, interconnected paths is an easy way to break up any amount of real estate into manageable garden plots. This makes selecting plants, planting, and

Seating areas, colorful plants, and garden art are connected by a winding gravel path.

maintaining each mini-garden much more manageable. Paths could be traditional gravel, concrete, flagstone, pavers, granite fines – even simple mulch. An advantage to gravel or mulch, however, is permeability. Because they allow water and air to percolate into the soil below, gravel and mulch walkways can be widened or redirected easily to incorporate mature trees or large shrubs into a new design when overly enthusiastic roots do not allow for under-planting. Regardless of the paving you choose, consider material in a shade of gold or tan, which contrasts pleasantly with the planted areas. As long as you use a consistent material throughout, the pathways will perform the same visually unifying function as a lawn.

Be cautious of inadvertently creating too many intersecting pathways, however, which will result in a chaotic, crowded-looking design. If, after laying out the new walkways, the resulting planting areas feel too large to comfortably maintain, consider adding what I think of as junior pathways. Instead of a path made from the same material as the major pathways, allow two or three broad stepping-stones to twine a few feet into a bed. These will also simplify maintenance and encourage a closer inspection of the garden.

For the mini-gardens themselves, rather than planting flat and flush with paths, take advantage of the smaller garden beds by shaping garden soil into mounds. These mounds, often referred to as berms, are an excellent way to vary the topography even in a small space, a particularly appealing feature while the garden is still filling in and the plants are small and uniform. Man-made mounds will gradually compact and settle over time, so plan on building them up to a greater height than what you ultimately want to wind up with. Berms are most attractive when they have a free-form shape, so rather than mounding them into perfectly conical anthills, vary their width and height. They are also a practical way to reuse any excess soil from the pathway excavation – just be sure to amend the soil with compost if the native soil is dense clay or lacking in nutrients. Finally, berms are also an excellent way to improve drainage, a particularly important consideration in gardens with heavy clay soil.

An appealing aspect of this design as a replacement for lawn is the opportunity it makes for creative play. Curving pathways make great play spaces for games where children chase each other, and are certainly exciting highways for tricycles. For older children, why not give them their own garden bed, to plant and care for as they choose?

Non-traditional lawns

Perhaps you want to keep the functionality and the look of a lawn, but want to reduce maintenance chores or dependency on supplemental water and chemicals. Fortunately, homeowners nationwide have been moving toward more sustainable options, which has led to the introduction of a range of lawn choices appropriate for different parts of the country.

opposite top Meandering paths wend through a no-lawn garden.

opposite bottom Seen from above, this curvy stroll garden shows off its strong lines.

A California native no-mow mix handles full sun and light foot traffic, while using 40 percent less water than traditional turf grass.

Not all lawn options perform equally, so before settling on one, take time to determine what your performance requirements are. Questions to ask include:

- How much foot traffic must the lawn be able to handle?
- Is water conservation an issue?
- How much maintenance am I willing to do?

Despite their ubiquity, most commonly used turf grasses, such as Kentucky bluegrass, zoysia, and tall fescues, are not native to any portion of the country, but in fact are European imports. For a long time, grass species like these were the only options available. Fortunately, in recent years growers and nurseries have developed native and ecological turf selections that are adapted for local growing conditions throughout North America. Traditional turf grass is usually a monoculture, meaning it is made up of a single type of plant. While this creates a uniform look, it also results in a lawn that performs well only in very specific situations. In contrast, ecological lawn alternatives are made up of a blend of native and adapted species. Mixed lawns like these are bred to perform better in specific regions of the country, and are designed

left Grass-like species in different heights create more variety and interest than a single expanse of lawn.

following page A blue grama (*Bouteloua gracilis*) grass meadow lawn requires only 8 to 9 inches of water a year, making it an excellent choice for this Arizona garden.

to thrive on minimal supplemental irrigation and fertilization. For the most part, they do not appreciate regular mowing (although there are some exceptions), which means that while they can be walked on comfortably, they shouldn't be mowed to the short, uniform height of a traditional lawn. While this makes them a poor choice for sports fields, their reduced maintenance requirements and regional appropriateness make them a smart choice for most backyard gardens.

Native and ecological lawns come the closest to replicating the look of a traditional lawn, but if all you are looking for is a swath of green that doesn't need to handle much foot traffic, numerous ground cover plants can work in place of grass. One challenge, however, is that they are generally only available for purchase in small sizes; most are sold as plugs or cell packs. Unlike traditional turf, which is either rolled out as sod for an instant lawn, or hydro-seeded for relatively fast results, ground covers planted as individual plants can take months to years to completely fill in. This can make weeding a more regular chore than most of us like. For that reason, I recommend limiting the size of a ground cover lawn and opting for species that fill in more quickly.

high-performing lawn alternative ground covers

Traditional turf grasses aren't the only options for achieving a lush sweep of manicured lawn. Though they can't handle the high foot traffic of sod, these ground covers offer some of the same advantages of turf grass, while using less water and providing more environmental benefits.

Plant	USDA zones	Description
'Coastal Gem' grevillea (*Grevillea lanigera* 'Coastal Gem')	9–10	A low-growing, mounding shrub, this attractive ground cover sports grayish green, needlelike foliage that stays evergreen all year round. Bi-colored flowers in shades of pink and white bloom almost continuously throughout the year.
Roman chamomile (*Chamaemelum nobile*)	4–9	The finely textured, rich green foliage of chamomile forms a solid mat and makes an excellent ground cover for a small area. Although its yellow flowers are inconspicuous, chamomile releases a heady herbal fragrance when stepped on or brushed against. Mow or shear occasionally.
'Elfin' thyme (*Thymus serpyllum* 'Elfin')	4–9	With small, closely spaced leaves and lilac-colored flowers that bloom in spring or summer, thyme is a classic choice for a lawnlet or between stepping-stones. May become leggy if it receives less than 5 hours of sun a day.
barren strawberry (*Waldsteinia fragarioides*)	4–7	This ornamental strawberry-like plant makes an attractive, leafy, semi-evergreen ground cover. Cheerful yellow flowers appear in late spring. It is not particularly tolerant of heat and humidity, making it a good choice for more northern climates.
creeping raspberry (*Rubus rolfei*)	6–10	Forms a dense mat and is equally at home cascading over ledges or terraces. It produces insignificant white flowers in spring and occasionally fruits in summer. The real attraction, however, is the fall foliage: textured, thumbnail-sized leaves that begin a medium green and turn bright red to deep burgundy.
'Catlin's Giant' carpet bugle (*Ajuga reptans* 'Catlin's Giant')	3–9	A low, mounding form and shiny, bronze-tinted leaves make this a good option for adding contrast and texture to shady areas. In early spring, bright blue flowers are held on short spikes above the foliage. An excellent option for compacted soils near mature trees. Plants die back somewhat in cold weather, but return with vigor in spring.

clockwise, from top left
'Coastal Gem' grevillea, Roman chamomile, barren strawberry, 'Catlin's Giant' carpet bugle, creeping raspberry, 'Elfin' thyme,

Artificial turf

Drought conditions and sporadic mandatory water rationing have played havoc on traditional lawns in the western United States. Not surprisingly, this has led to increased interest in artificial turf as a no-water, evergreen alternative. Indeed, synthetic turf does provide some advantages over living lawn. It liberates you entirely from the tyranny of weekly mowing, not to mention semi-annual applications of fertilizer, yearly aeration, and the ongoing need to monitor and maintain irrigation. In the past, artificial turf was manufactured in a uniform green, but most products on the market today are significantly more natural looking — manufacturers have added in patches of brown or thatch, and offer grass blades that mimic specific lawn species. Where you place artificial turf can also affect how realistic it looks. Avoid the temptation to keep the lawn pristine, and instead allow some debris from nearby trees and plants to fall on it. You may have heard concerns about lead content; these relate to artificial turf manufactured before 2009, not to currently produced varieties.

On the downside, if you are choosing artificial turf for a sunny play space, be aware that unlike grass, it heats up when exposed to direct, hot sun. Manufacturers are beginning to address this by designing newer versions with some heat reflecting

As irrigation is not required, synthetic turf can be cut into a variety of shapes to accommodate a design.

ability—worth looking into if you live in a warmer climate zone. Synthetic lawns are also not completely free of maintenance; they must be regularly rinsed down to stay clean, which in parts of the country with limited rainfall means hosing them down by hand. Areas that become mildly or heavily soiled must be sponge mopped with the cleaner recommended for the type of the stain. Tree sap, animal waste, and mold all have the ability to discolor artificial turf. In addition to cleaning, regular brushing is required to keep artificial grass from flattening out, especially in high traffic areas.

Environmentally, artificial turf earns a mainly neutral score. While it does not adversely affect the environment while it's in place, neither does it offer any benefits. Unlike plant species—including traditional turf—that have the ability to sequester carbon, filter stormwater, and even provide pollen or food for insects and wildlife, artificial lawns don't contribute to planetary or neighborhood health. As is true for many synthetic products, once your lawn has completed its useful lifespan, it cannot be recycled—it must be taken to a landfill.

Considering Views

If you limit yourself to creating a garden design from a bird's-eye view, you risk ending up with a garden that looks beautiful on paper but is less than ideal once constructed. It's equally important to imagine yourself walking through the space, and to create a view plan based on what you will be able to see as you do. Both are helpful ways of visualizing your space, and I encourage you to consider each perspective as you create or renovate your garden. I usually start by making at least a rough sketch of where the most important features will be, then I balance this with a 3-D perspective. Positioning the garden's primary elements (such as patios, lawns, and planting beds) via a plan view sketch is important for establishing the right scale, managing circulation, and also for ensuring that each area is appropriately sized for whatever activities it needs to accommodate. Incorporating a third dimension allows you to understand how areas within the garden relate to one another as they will actually be used, as well as how the backyard interacts with the house and surrounding scenery.

Incorporating views is particularly important in small backyards, as it adds yet another layer to the garden. But where and how do you create views? To keep from getting overwhelmed during the design process and to make sure you highlight the garden's most important attributes, establish a hierarchy of views. Begin with wherever you plan to spend the majority of your time. For most of us, that will be on a primary patio or deck located just outside the back door. Where will the furniture go? Can it be oriented to look toward the most attractive aspects of the garden? If not, can or should the garden be redesigned in the places that will be seen? In addition to establishing pleasant views, are there any unsightly areas that should be hidden, or that suggest rethinking the placement of the patio itself? It's normal for some of your answers to these questions to fall into a gray area. Furnishings and structures like stand-alone barbecues and storage sheds may not be intrinsically unappealing, but if they inadvertently dominate a key view and block more attractive garden areas, consider adjusting your design.

Other views to consider are those that open up as you walk along and around the pathways, as well as any secondary activity areas your garden includes. Views from within the house should be considered too! Finally, think about how the spaces you create will be influenced by their proximity to your backyard's fences or by what you can see beyond your property line.

The Art of the Focal Point

Emphasizing views allows you to actively shape how your garden will be experienced. To better understand this, imagine your garden as a movie, and yourself as its director. During filming, the director's goal is not just to tell a story but also to influence how the audience will react by setting mood. A director uses direction—and sometimes misdirection—to point us toward what he or she wants us to see, think, or even feel. By considering things besides just the basics of plants and hardscape, you become a director in the most literal sense. As such, one of your most effective tools for directing views is the thoughtful selection and placement of focal points. Focal points are generally defined as unique visual accents or elements, such as a fountain, bench, or standout plant, that draw the eye. But not all focal points function in the same way. Before siting any garden décor, consider what you hope to accomplish.

Lead the eye

A beautiful garden is like a painted composition, and well-placed focal points give it interest and visual balance. In a small garden, visitors rarely need help navigating the garden in a literal sense, but there is still an opportunity to influence the way they interact within the space. Strategically placed focal points attract and arrest attention, providing a space for the eye to pause before moving in to explore. Because a progression of carefully considered focal points allows a garden's beauty to be revealed at a gradual pace, anything that forces a pause is a boon to a small garden, where the tendency is for a visitor to try to digest what he or she can see all at once.

Virtually any object can act as a focal point, as long as it stands out from what surrounds it. For collectors of plants, containers, or outdoor art, focal point placement is particularly crucial. When objects designed to invite contemplation are lumped too closely together, the result can be visual chaos or the risk that no single item can be appreciated for its uniqueness. Conversely, when scattered thoughtfully throughout the garden, inherently interesting objects become an invitation to stop

top left Tall, vertical art pieces that contrast with surrounding foliage make excellent garden focal points.

left Placed at the back of the garden, "Bird Lady" helps guide the eye through the space.

top right Garden statuary is a time-honored choice for a focal point in a traditional garden.

above Smaller pieces of art that are best admired at close range make attractive focal points near patios or other spaces where people congregate.

for a moment before moving on. Each object helps define the character or mood of its own little piece of garden. If you have room for more than one focal point, avoid the urge to line them up rigidly or space them equidistant from one another – the result will be that they look like a matched set connected to each other, rather than to the space they inhabit in the garden. A placement that is slightly off center or more organic encourages the eye to move in more than one direction, once again slowing down the pace at which the garden's features are absorbed.

Consider the scale of objects and plants before you decide on a permanent placement for them in the garden. Small or intricate pieces work better close to seating areas or pathways where their detail can be appreciated. Statuary and plants that are farther away should be large enough to be understood at a distance, although conversely, if the object hints that a closer inspection will be rewarded with additional details, this invites visitors to range deeper into the garden. The choice of focal points may not be entirely under your control, however. If your backyard possesses a large or distinctive tree, for example, it will typically become a focal point by default. If this is the case, feel free to celebrate its prominence by adding a birdhouse, wind chime, or other type of garden enhancement. This is a particularly desirable approach for trees or large shrubs with a short season of interest.

Unify a space

On field trips in my student days, we often asked the instructors to point out various real-life examples of design principles. Whenever one of our teachers was asked to identify the unifying element in a garden, "the lawn" was his inevitable response. I wasn't quite sure that was a satisfying answer at the time, and now that I see so many homeowners choosing to minimize or remove lawns altogether, I've begun noticing and creating other ways to make a garden feel cohesive. Focal point placement works as an excellent strategy for connecting two or more spaces visually. Placing an object that is attractive when viewed from multiple sides (such as a circular water feature, small tree, or oversized urn) between multiple activity areas simultaneously creates both a subtle connection and a division. Activity areas are defined while remaining integrated. This works with multiple layouts, but is particularly effective with L-shaped patios, as placing an object with mass in the right angle created by the patio's inside corner helps relieve the flatness of the surrounding hardscape.

Focal points can also be created from more than one object. This is particularly true if you are dividing a large expanse of continuous hardscape. In this instance, a lone object might appear too isolated, but a grouping of ornaments – such as containers of different heights with a similar finish or material – could work beautifully. Be sure to keep the grouping fairly cohesive and simple; for example, three containers of similar material, but no more.

Bring the outdoors in

Using focal points to create and guide views can be expanded to encompass more than just vistas within the garden itself. In fact, one of the most overlooked ways to get the most impact out of a small garden is to make it function like living wallpaper for your home's interior. Windows often become default focal points inside a home, because the movement and color of the garden beyond naturally draw the eye. Make the outside view a prominent window showcases even more effective by anchoring the view with a focal point. This does not need to be distinct from focal point trees or objects you've already chosen — use whatever you've already decided should unify the garden. But when considering the placement of any new elements outdoors, factor in which windows or glass doors in your home overlook the backyard, and adjust the locations of newly introduced objects to create pleasing vistas from inside the house.

Glass doors frame a garden view dominated by an elegantly twisted oak.

A birdbath in the foreground acts as anchoring contrast to the view of surrounding hills.

Borrowed Scenery

The standard advice for laying out small gardens is to focus on blocking undesirable views and planting trees or incorporating garden structures to ensure privacy. While this can be a good idea, rather than shutting out the space that lies beyond your property line, consider incorporating the extended environment into your own design if at all possible. The Japanese word *shakkei* is often translated as "borrowed scenery," and refers to the design principle of incorporating the surrounding landscape into your garden composition. Desirable scenery can range from something as grand as distant mountains, a city skyline, or even a well-planted golf course to something as simple as an attractive tree in your neighbor's garden. Using taller shrubs and trees to frame desirable views essentially extends the walls of your own garden — at no additional cost to you. If views are entirely open rather than glimpsed through structures and trees, consider adding low-growing plants in your garden to help anchor the space and further accentuate the frame.

Instead of fencing them out, incorporate the surrounding views into your design.

Neighboring yards don't need to have obvious focal-point plantings to factor into your design strategy, however. Note the location, size, color, and habit of the trees that border your own property. These can—and should—impact your plant choices for your own yard. If your neighbor has planted evergreen trees close to your shared border, for example, don't just plant more in an effort to make the palette consistent. Why not choose a tree with silver or burgundy leaves for your side of the fence, essentially taking advantage of their landscaping choices to create an attractive background that will be a visual foil for your own? Likewise, note any seasonal highlights in their backyard that are visible in yours. If your neighbor has chosen trees for spring blooms or fall color, take advantage of that in your own planting strategy.

the sensory garden

Have you ever visited a garden that at first glance seemed attractive and well maintained, yet after a short time left you feeling disinclined to linger and explore? A backyard may be beautifully designed, with attractive patios and pathways and well-shaped planting beds, yet leave us feeling flat and disengaged. Although beginning the design process with an overall layout plan is a good idea, if the process stops with only what can be communicated via a drawing, a lackluster garden can be the result. That's because a drawing alone neglects to capture the most important thing that sets the outdoor world apart from the indoors, and distinguishes residential backyards from residential interiors — that fact that gardens are *alive*.

Fragrant lavender and lemon tree blossoms perfume the garden.

We can learn more about this phenomenon from our pets. Take a close look at how your pets respond to being outside. Cats in particular are notorious for pausing in open doorways, half in one space and half in another. This can be partly chalked up to general feline quirkiness, but look closely at what puss is really doing. Notice how her nose quivers and ears twitch forward, eyes intently moving from space to space? She's taking time to drink in the sounds and scents of the garden, carefully noting everything in motion, down to the tiniest detail.

While a leaf blowing across the patio or a lizard scampering up a wall might not captivate us as completely, our enjoyment of being outside is enhanced by a space brimming with sound, movement, color, and scent. Fortunately, it's actually easier to make these things prominent and noticeable in a garden that's not overly large.

At the most basic level, the technical act of simply adding plants to a backyard creates life. But the savvy homeowner goes beyond that, and actively seeks out the aromatic plants, colorful accessories and clever layout strategies that will create an environment alive with activity, regardless of the area's size. To unwind on a patio while birds call, leaves rustle in the breeze, and the heady perfume of scented flowers fills the air, is to immerse yourself in an in-the-moment experience unique to being outside. There's a reason spending time outdoors is known as one of the best stress-busting activities, but it only works if our backyards are truly infused with nature. Sterile concrete slabs and precisely clipped hedges won't feed our senses or evoke the serenity necessary to distance us from the built-up urban environment and relentless pace that marks so much of our days. That's why it's so important to include the elements of movement, sound, color and scent in every garden: these dynamic, sensual features reveal how alive a garden really is and keep us feeling alive too!

Pets are often more proficient than their owners in exploring a garden with all five senses.

The Sound and Movement of Water

One of the most effective ways to introduce movement and sound into a garden is with water. Every culture throughout history has included water as an essential element in gardens. The paradise gardens created thousands of years ago by ancient desert civilizations – and immortalized in the design of traditional Persian carpets – included canals or ponds and were typically organized around a central water source. Similarly, Greek villas and medieval cloisters generally feature a wellhead or fountain right in the middle. The connection between water and gardens continues today. Whether in small ways like a modest backyard fountain, or more dramatic features like cascading water walls, water has endured as a quintessential feature of contemporary landscape design precisely because of the dynamism it can add.

Although the illusion of water can be invoked by suggesting its form or color via plants and landscape accessories, when possible, including a real water element

is particularly rewarding and enjoyable. Besides being beautiful in and of itself, the sparkle of water in the sun attracts other life to a garden. A shallow dish placed where butterflies can enjoy a drink, a birdbath that provides respite for migrating birds, or a modest pond that can be home to lazy koi and deep-throated frogs all reinforce water's life-giving properties and enrich the garden experience. Watching birds splash around in a fountain is a guaranteed stress buster and mood lifter.

Homeowners sometimes shy away from water features, fearing they mean a lot of maintenance, but there are ways to take advantage of their benefits while minimizing chores. First, think small. Large ponds with cascading waterfalls can be expensive to install properly and maintain, and are generally too big to fit comfortably in a small backyard anyway. Just like swimming pools, they can be water wasters due to evaporation, making them less desirable in parts of the country prone to drought. If you have your heart set on the look and sound of a significant water feature, consider one without a pond. While still providing the sound and presence of a moving body of water, pondless systems are based on a gravel-filled reservoir instead of a traditional pool liner, significantly reducing evaporation and maintenance.

An even more practical choice for most homeowners is a small fountain that sits atop an in-ground reservoir. Fountains like this can be purchased prefabricated, or you can make one from a container, slab of stone, or anything that can have a hole drilled through the bottom of it. Installing this type of fountain entails burying a sealed waterproof container below ground, with a grate on top that the water feature rests on. Decorative rock and gravel cover the grate, and the water that spills from the fountain is re-circulated via a pump in the reservoir. Burying the mechanical elements helps integrate the fountain with the rest of the garden, creating a natural effect. While not nearly as expensive or maintenance intensive as a pond, in-ground reservoirs do have a somewhat complex installation process and because their pump

left The sparkle of moving water attracts birds flying overhead.

above A jar fountain with a covered top is safe for birds to land on.

and reservoir are buried below grade, take more effort to maintain than units that sit entirely above ground.

The easiest option by far is a self-contained, jar-style fountain. These sit in a saucer and feature an integrated, internal pump, so they require minimal effort to install and very little maintenance other than topping off the water and an occasional cleaning. Instead of being open like a traditional, tiered fountain container, a jar fountain is semi-enclosed on top; this helps keep it clean inside and more important, provides an appealing landing place for the songbirds that will be attracted to the sparkle of the water. If you fall in love with a container at a nursery and want to make your own self-contained fountain, keep it bird friendly by topping the jar with a piece of plexiglass with a hole drilled in the center. Cover that sheet with a layer of gravel and a few larger stones—this will not only create a more attractive feature, but will help birds gauge the depth and land more safely. Jar fountains provide more movement and sparkle than sound, since the water doesn't splash. If the sound of lapping or falling water is important to you, opt for a tiered-style fountain.

Your water feature's placement is critical. Unlike a specimen tree or piece of art that is often placed farther out in the landscape as a focal point, fountains are ideally enjoyed up close. Besides creating a soothing burbling sound of their own, water features can serve the practical purpose of masking other noise, whether that's minimizing the sound of a neighbor's lawn mower or keeping your own backyard conversations private. They can only do this effectively if they are located near primary

A small, rustic fountain with an in-ground reservoir bubbles amid surrounding greenery.

opposite Situate a fountain close enough to a seating area that the sight and sound of water can be enjoyed.

Trailing rosemary mimics the flow of water.

opposite A dry creek bed paved with river rock suggests the presence of water.

seating areas or where people will congregate. If welcoming wildlife into your yard is one of your goals, know that birds flying overhead are attracted to the shimmer of moving water, so avoid locating your fountain under a dense tree or anything that shields it from overhead view.

Creating the illusion of water

In smaller gardens, it may be impossible or undesirable to include actual water in a garden. An alternative is to represent water's fluidity and movement in other ways. Planting a swath of the same plant in an informal curved drift, for example, will evoke the sense of flowing water. Ornamental grasses are ideal for adding movement to a garden, as their elegant plumes sway in even the lightest breeze. These grasses also act as light catchers the same way water does, in that they capture and enhance the glow of the sun, particularly when backlit in mornings or late afternoons.

In nature, water of course moves not only horizontally, via streams and rivers, but also from one vertical level to another as it cascades down hillsides and mountains. Mimicking the look of waterfalls with plants that trail or drape evocatively from window boxes, retaining walls, or over the lips of containers can suggest the movement and flow of water, particularly if you choose specimens with blue-toned or silvery foliage or blooms.

Curving landscape features also suggest movement, and can be a low-maintenance way to make a space more dynamic. Try creating a "stream" of river rock or decorative gravel that meanders through the garden. If you're willing to commit to a permanent feature, consider carving a pebble or mosaic ribbon into existing hardscape to introduce the sinuous shape of moving water.

plants to create the illusion of water

Water is one of the most pleasing elements to add to a small garden, but when a water feature is impractical, an alternative is to incorporate plants that mimic water's graceful flow. Plants that drape loosely over walls, sport gracefully arching foliage, or bloom in blue hues bring a similar sense of movement and fluidity to the garden.

Plant	USDA zones	Description
Cape Mendocino reed grass (*Calamagrostis foliosa*)	8–9	In summer, arching wheat-colored flowers that droop gracefully complement the blue sheen of the leaves. Reaches 1 to 2 feet high and wide.
lavender (*Lavandula* spp.)	5–9	Fragrant spikes of pale to dark blue flowers are held above aromatic, gray-green foliage.
ROZANNE geranium (*Geranium* 'Gerwat' ROZANNE)	5–9	Its long blooming season, blue flowers, and mounding, billowy habit makes this a wonderful choice to spill over the edge of a pathway. 1 to 2 feet high and 2 to 4 feet wide.
creeping rosemary (*Rosmarinus officinalis* spp.)	8–10	Hardy and fast growing, prostrate forms of rosemary such as 'Prostratus', 'Irene', and 'Huntington Carpet' drape attractively over walls and from containers. 1 to 2 feet high and 4 to 8 feet wide.
'Beyond Blue' fescue (*Festuca glauca* 'Beyond Blue')	4–9	Unusually bright blue foliage and compact size make this cultivar a small-space standout. Notable for maintaining its blue color nearly year-round in milder climates. 12 inches high and 18 inches wide.
beargrass (*Nolina texana*)	7–10	With needlelike, muddy-green leaves that tend to settle into a puddle, beargrass is particularly effective at mimicking water when allowed to tumble over the side of a wall. 3 feet high and 3 to 4 feet wide.

clockwise, from top left
Cape Mendocino reed grass, lavender, creeping rosemary, beargrass, 'Beyond Blue' fescue, ROZANNE geranium

Attracting wildlife

One of the great pleasures of being in nature is having close encounters with the denizens of a healthy, vibrant ecosystem. Lush backyards are not only wonderful to look at and spend time in, they have the potential to attract wildlife. Like water, birds, bees, and butterflies add movement and sound to a garden, and while they can't be controlled per se, the charm of interacting with them often stems from their unpredictability. Part of the enjoyment of being outdoors is hoping for and then relishing unexpected visits, which always feel like a gift. Creating gardens that are attractive to wildlife is especially rewarding in small spaces, where you are generally only a few feet from the action.

Of all the critters that can be encouraged to visit a garden, pollinators are among the most valuable. This term encompasses any animal, bird, or insect that helps plants produce fruit or seeds. They do this by moving pollen from the flowers of one plant to another, thereby fertilizing them. Without pollinators, plants cannot reproduce. Of course, there are other species of wildlife you may want to attract to your garden, but the great thing about pollinators is that with a little encouragement in the right direction, they'll visit just about any garden. You don't need to live in the country or have a large property. Your garden can be as small as a few containers on a balcony—if planted correctly, you can count on visitors. In fact, in densely populated urban areas, container gardens can play an important environmental role because food sources for birds and insects can be far between. Think of city balconies and courtyards as an important part of an urban wildlife corridor that creates spaces for birds and insects to rest or stop for a snack.

Long-blooming blanket flower (*Gaillardia* spp.) makes a bright addition to a pollinator garden.

Bees and butterflies

There are numerous insects that act as pollinators, but bees are probably the most well known, as they are among the most prolific and important. When a bee lands on a flower to drink its nectar, it comes into contact with a plant's pollen sacs. As the bee flies off, some of this pollen is carried away with it, making it available as fertilizer for the next flower it visits. This process of cross-pollination helps at least 30 percent of the world's crops and 90 percent of wild plants to thrive. In home gardens, bees play an important role as pollinators of popular traditional fruits and vegetables, like apples, cranberries, melons, and blueberries.

Many balk at actively encouraging these gentle creatures for fear of painful stings, but unless you are highly allergic, this concern is unwarranted. Bees are provoked to attack only when they perceive their colony is in danger and needs protecting. A bee will rarely sting when out foraging for food or water.

Beyond their importance in food production and plant health, bees are one of the most attractive visitors in the garden to simply sit back and observe. They provide a sensory experience unique to the outdoors. Most of us are familiar with

the slender shape and muted gold and black stripes of a European honeybee, if only from the pictures illustrating the squeeze bottles of honey in the grocery store. But it doesn't take much time in a garden friendly to pollinators to discover there are a host of other bees waiting to entertain us as they go about their business. In fact, one of my favorite backyard visitors is the carpenter bee, whose appearance is about as far from the fast-flitting, smaller honeybee as you can get. Pitch black and an inch long, twice the size of their zippier cousins, carpenter bees can be a little startling if you've never seen one up close before. But once you are accustomed to their misleadingly fierce looks, you'll find that few things are as relaxing as sitting down and watching the slow, methodical flight of these gentle giants as they glide from flower to flower. Their low-pitched hum has the same calming effect as waves washing up on an ocean's shore.

Butterflies are less controversial visitors—pollinators that almost everyone enjoys seeing in the garden. Because of their long, thin legs and lack of specialized structures for collecting pollen, they are not as efficient as bees at cross-fertilization, although they still play an important role. Despite being less effective at attaching pollen to their bodies, they do boast superior eyesight, meaning they can perceive bright colors such as red more easily. Additionally, their longer legs allow them to pollinate larger flowers. But there's no need to choose between trying to attract bees or butterflies; for the most part, they prefer the same garden conditions.

There are several things you can do to encourage pollinators in your garden. The easiest is to include nectar- and pollen-rich plants, to provide food sources. Good options are long-flowering plants like agastache (*Agastache* spp.), blanket flower (*Gaillardia* spp.), and cosmos (*Cosmos bipinnatus*). While bees collect pollen from a wide range of plants, they are especially attracted to plants whose blooms, upon close inspection, are actually made up of many small, individual flowers. A good example is common yarrow (*Achillea* spp.), which is equally inviting to butterflies as its wide, flat flowers make an excellent landing pad.

left Beardtongue (*Penstemon* spp.) is an exceptional plant choice for attracting bees.

above Meadow blazingstar (*Liatris ligulistylis*) is a magnet for butterflies.

pollinators and insecticides

Use caution when shopping for pollinator plants and make sure you know how they were grown. Neonicotinoids are a broad category of insecticides that are frequently used to keep young plants free from damage by pests. Unfortunately, some studies indicate they may contribute to colony collapse disorder, a phenomenon that occurs when too many adult bees leave the hive, making it difficult for the queen and immature bees to survive. The pesticide is absorbed by a plant's pollen. Although many growers avoid spraying neonicotinoids while plants are in bloom, this only avoids immediate honeybee death. The pesticide may remain in the plant for several years, so when bees bring pollen back to the hive, it has the potential to build into a concentrate that weakens and may ultimately kill the hive. If you are choosing plants specifically for their ability to attract pollinators, search out online retailers that avoid the practice, or consult with your local garden center to determine the pollinator safety of the plants they are carrying.

'African Blue' basil is an excellent example of a plant that does triple duty in small gardens. Besides attracting pollinators over a lengthy bloom season, flowering does not turn the leaves bitter, making it a particularly long-lasting culinary herb.

Many other plants besides perennials are attractive to pollinators. Fruit trees as well as traditional landscape trees such as maple, black locust, and pepper also attract bees. Larger landscape trees like these can be especially desirable if your garden has the space, because colonies will visit en masse when the tree is in flower. If listening to a few bees flit about the garden is similar to enjoying a cat's purr, then sitting under the canopy of a tree covered with honeybees is like being surrounded by an entire litter of contented kittens.

Beyond flowers, trees, and shrubs, bees and butterflies are attracted to many types of edible plants. Numerous traditional herbs lure pollinators, including basil, mint, thyme, chives, sage, and oregano. The key, of course, is to allow at least some of the herbs to flower. Although standard culinary herbs work just fine, if you want to take your herb garden and pollinator stewardship to the next level, consider 'African Blue' basil. It flowers early in the season, sporting stunning blue-black stems of small purple flowers that are irresistible to bees and can also be used as garnish in salads. Unlike the leaves of many culinary types of basil, 'African Blue' foliage does not become bitter when the plant is allowed to flower, making this a terrific herb to share.

How you care for your pollinator garden is equally as important as what you plant. It is crucial that you take an organic approach and avoid any pesticides or herbicides. Many of the chemicals found in them are toxic to pollinators.

You can also simplify yard maintenance chores by encouraging or introducing beneficial insects. Indoors, we tend to lump all insects into the same "undesirable and uninvited" category, but this is not true outdoors, where some insects actively participate in the health of a garden. These beneficial insects can fight nuisance insects, which can damage plants and even limit our ability to enjoy the outdoors due to aggressive behavior and the tendency to sting. For example, while there is no safe way of chemically eradicating the annoying aphids that are munching on your roses without also killing off the bugs you'd like to keep around, you can introduce a squad of ladybugs (*Hippodamia convergens*) to combat them. In fact, one ladybug can eat an impressive 5000 aphids in its one-year lifespan. What the ladybugs don't get, you can spray off with a hose. Not to be outdone, the soldier beetle (*Podisus maculiventris*) is as ferocious as its name implies, and preys on nearly a hundred different garden pests. Ultimately, resisting the urge to wage chemical warfare will result in less maintenance and a much healthier garden.

Hummingbirds

Hummingbirds pollinate a variety of shrubs and flowers, and like bees, are important to wild flower pollination. They are attracted to nectar-producing plants, and their long beaks are particularly adept at seeking out the nectar hidden inside bell-shaped blooms like those of flowering maple (*Abutilon* spp.). You can also attract hummers with specialized hanging feeders, although in general, even feeders kept full of artificial nectar provide less than 25 percent of their nutritional needs, so adding plants that are a food source will greatly increase your chances of having these beautiful and entertaining birds visit your garden. If you do add a feeder or two, be kind and makes sure at least one has a place to perch — it's a myth that they only feed while in flight.

Cardinal flower (*Lobelia cardinalis*) is irresistible to hummingbirds.

Good choices for attracting hummingbirds include cardinal flower (*Lobelia cardinalis*), trumpet honeysuckle (*Lonicera sempervirens*), and trumpet creeper (*Campsis radicans*). If you want to attract a nesting pair and try to entice them to stick around, there are several things you can do. At least one tree is essential – they build their nests anywhere from 10 to 90 feet off the ground. A selection of shrubs will provide them with the twigs and bits of leaves they need to build their tiny nests, which are bound together with spider silk. Parent birds need tiny spiders and bugs to feed their offspring, so resist the urge to exterminate your local arachnid or insect populations. Beyond their environmental benefit as pollinators, hummingbirds' good looks and crazy antics make them particularly attractive garden visitors. It is impossible not to admire these birds' iridescent plumage; it shines like precious jewels. But what really makes a hummer special is its cocky personality. While hummingbirds typically weigh about as much as two pennies, they seem completely oblivious to their diminutive size and frequently challenge much larger birds. In the same way a toy poodle will bark out a fearless challenge to a bigger dog, it is common for male hummers to stake out a patch of garden and guard it zealously. Highly territorial, the pitched battle of aggressive males over ownership of a feeder or a desirable feeding ground is as entertaining as any action movie, and in modest-sized gardens, it's like having a front row seat.

Color

Color is one of the most important design elements of any indoor room, but fewer homeowners think about color being equally essential to the spaces we create outside. Not only can the judicious use of color have a huge visual impact, it also has the ability to directly affect our moods. The color red, for example, has the power to raise blood pressure, while the color green stimulates the pituitary gland and helps keep both our minds and bodies relaxed. Incorporating personal color preferences into a garden makes them – and the experience of creating them – uniquely our own.

While there is no doubt that flowers add spectacular color to a landscape, it is also true that maintaining annuals – as well as perennials to a lesser extent – is a labor-intensive aspect of having a garden, and not necessarily in keeping with the less is more approach to gardening. With annuals, you have the option to mix things up by choosing something different every year, but that also means purchasing and replanting plants every year. Perennials live longer, but also often require deadheading, cutting back or even dividing every few years, chores that many would rather minimize. For all these reasons, it's good to think about additional strategies for incorporating long-term, low-maintenance color in the garden in addition to flowers and foliage.

Besides traditional methods such as accessories and flowers, color can be introduced into the garden via a home's exterior walls.

The easiest way to do this is with accessories such as cushions, bright containers, or furniture such as chairs and benches. Often overlooked, however, is the opportunity to play with color using a garden's permanent structural elements; fences, walls, gates, and arbors all provide opportunities to create a unique color story. A fence's main job might be to maintain privacy or keep out deer, but that doesn't mean it can't double as an art project. Adding color to your garden's decorative fixtures also means that you can have color year-round. This is particularly appealing for colder climates, where much of a garden's foliage goes dormant or is covered by snow in winter.

I always recommend taking a light hand with large features, such as fences and walls. Choose a soft or neutral color for these backdrops. If you're attracted to stronger colors, use them as accents or in concentrated areas, as too many bright colors can overwhelm a small space (although like all design guidelines, there are exceptions). Just as you might paint one accent wall inside the house, choose one or two outdoor surfaces to call out.

If a fence is older and in poor condition—or, conversely, if it's already stained but you want to add more color—it might not be practical or desirable to paint just one part of it. Overlaying a painted wood panel in front of one or more sections of a fence, however, is a relatively easy way to add a pop of color, with the added benefit that the effect is less permanent. Make sure you choose a wood for the panel that stands up well to the outdoors, such as cedar or pine, and choose exterior-grade paint.

Color certainly brings a shot of personal style into a garden, but it also strongly influences how a garden is experienced. Color specialists theorize that certain colors evoke universal reactions. Being aware of this can help you emphasize (or de-emphasize) specific features in your garden. For example, blue inspires calmness and relaxation, so it would be an excellent choice for an area set aside for reading, meditating, or quiet conversation. Hot colors like red and orange draw the eye, making them a good option for accents or focal points. Their eye-catching nature means they can also be employed to draw attention away from less desirable areas of the garden, such as compost bins or storage areas, which in limited-space gardens can't always be completely hidden. They can even serve as a distraction for unappealing views.

Creating your color story

There are many resources available to people redecorating a home's interior in a particular color scheme. But other than catalog photos of outdoor furniture, pages torn from magazines, or user-driven websites like Pinterest or Houzz, there aren't a lot of places for homeowners to get ideas on how to add color to a landscape effectively, which can make the process intimidating. Following one of the strategies below will help you combine colors in a way that's cohesive.

A hot pink panel provides a vibrant backdrop to a container filled with succulents.

A mix of textures, plants, and accessories in a limited palette of greens makes this monochromatic garden a standout.

Go monochromatic

If your tastes run to clean, bold, or simple, or you are simply gaga for one specific color, opt for a monochromatic approach. Choose a single hue to use as your inspiration, and repeat it throughout the garden with both plants and accents. This is a particularly effective strategy for contemporary garden designs, which are often associated with clean color profiles. It also works well for gardens that already have a lot going on architecturally speaking, as it allows individual hardscape elements to shine and ensures that color clutter won't overwhelm a smaller garden.

Purchasing unfinished wood containers and painting them yourself allows you to determine a consistent color palette in advance.

Choose your palette in advance

Nailing down the colors you want to emphasize before you start a color transformation will ensure a harmonious result, while still allowing room for impulse buys like containers and cushions. Once you're certain you like the way a color looks in your garden, you can work on increasing its presence a little at a time. And don't limit yourself to what you can find online or in a garden center—wood containers can be custom built or ordered prefabricated in a range of sizes online, which gives you the option of painting them yourself. This makes it much easier to choose a color palette that is as sophisticated, soft, or whimsical as you like. While furniture and outdoor accessory manufacturers offer only a handful of colors, paint stores carry an almost unlimited range. This approach is a great time-saver as well, as a trip to the paint store and an afternoon spent painting is a more manageable process than multiple trips to garden centers, in search of the perfect containers.

Follow a theme

There are many ways to come up with a color story that works for you. If your garden was inspired by a specific style or other single idea, let that guide your color choices. Tropical-themed gardens, for example, are popular in many parts of the

country, not just where tropical plants would naturally grow. A garden that pops with vivid shades of orange, red, and yellow in flowers native to a range of climates will evoke a cheerful vacation mood in your backyard. In fact, travel is a common source of inspiration for many of my clients. Since our gardens are often used to unwind and relax, they are the perfect place to try recreating a favorite vacation destination, if only in a small way. Distant places we hope to visit one day but have not managed to get to yet can also influence our gardens – the whole point is to let your backyard transport you away from your daily surroundings. You don't have to have spent time in the French or Italian countryside to be able to appreciate their charm. Walls painted in soft ochre, combined with lavender-colored containers, can evoke the spirit of the Mediterranean in your own suburban backyard.

Choose two complementary colors

Colors that sit opposite each other on the color wheel are considered complementary. Aesthetically speaking, a color's complement provides its best contrast. Incorporating this type of color strategy into the garden requires a thoughtful approach; too much contrast can be a little garish when viewed year-round. Think how unrestful your interior would be if you decorated it in complementary red and green holiday colors year-round. In general, if you would like to use very saturated, bright colors, such as yellow and purple, it is better to combine them sparingly, as accents, or to use them in planting combinations rather than drench the garden with them, as they can draw too much attention from other garden elements. An alternative – and one that often results in more sophisticated-looking gardens – is to choose softer, more natural shades of complementary colors. Soft gold and muted teal, for example, provide a harmonious but gentle contrast that won't overpower a small space.

left Subtler complementary hues such as teal and warm gold make a softer statement than primary colors.

above A favorite memory, such as a tropical vacation, can work as your color inspiration.

following page Complementary color pairings are most effective when used sparingly in plant combinations.

Building a garden around analogous colors—those that sit next to one another on the color wheel—is a great way to introduce a bold mix of colors that still play well together.

Explore analogous colors

Colors that reside adjacent to each other on the color wheel are known as analogous colors, and they offer an opportunity to create a pleasing range of tones that seem to slide naturally from one to the next without jarring juxtapositions. A cool palette of yellow-green, green, and blue-green, for example, would work well if you are planning on incorporating lots of green, leafy shrubs. A warmer palette of orange, red-orange, and deep red is a classic choice for a Mediterranean-style garden built around terra-cotta tiles and textured stucco walls. Using an analogous color grouping as your design roadmap gives you a wide range of colors to play with, while keeping your design cohesive.

Echo your plants

The walls, furnishings, and accessories in our gardens don't exist independently from the plants. If you've already created a garden with foliage and bloom colors that you find pleasing, why not continue to emphasize those colors by repeating them in other materials? Keep in mind that strong shades like deep crimsons and vivid blues attract the eye and act as natural focal points. Too many competing pops of bright color can be too much in a small space. Save this strategy for gardens with more subdued palettes that emphasize foliage over a wide range of flower color.

Scent

Our sense of smell plays an important role in our well-being. Considered by many to be the most primal of our senses, it influences memory, mood, and emotion. Think back to an outdoor experience that was meaningful to you. Was it a summer at the beach, or perhaps a family camping trip? Chances are, when you encounter scents associated with those particular memories — the tang of salt water or the sharp astringency of pine needles — those memories will involuntary resurface.

That's why scent can do so much to enhance the experience of being in a garden. A garden is a living, breathing ecosystem, and few things cater to the pleasure of fragrance better than flowers. Because it's easier to "trap" scent in a smaller area, adding only one or two fragrant plants may be all that you need. Getting the most sensory pleasure out of your garden, however, does mean choosing scented plants with an eye toward how you use the garden and when you will spend time in it. If you enjoy spending evenings outdoors, plants like night-blooming jasmine (*Cestrum nocturnum*) and evening stock (*Matthiola incana*) release their fragrance after dark. Conversely, if one of your goals is to bring the aromas of the garden indoors, create a cutting garden that includes scented plants that hold up well after they're harvested, such as hyacinth (*Hyacinthus orientalis*), freesia (*Freesia corymbosa*), or lilac (*Syringa* spp.).

'Cupani' sweet pea (*Lathyrus odoratus* 'Cupani') is an old-fashioned variety that is more fragrant than many newer cultivars.

Scented flowers vary widely in the intensity and quality of their fragrance. Much like you may have a signature perfume or cologne, plants that are intensely fragrant can create an equally personal statement in your garden. If you are looking for plants strong enough to perfume more than just their immediate area, choose a flowering shrub or a small tree over perennials and annuals. Trees and shrubs are an efficient choice for small spaces as well because one deliciously fragrant selection, such as a mock orange, will be enough to perfume the garden through the entire spring season. Where you plant will also impact how you perceive a scent. Plants close to the house will waft in with the breeze; if you want to perfume an area of your yard so you will smell it while you're reading in a certain chair, for example, plant that area so it is somewhat enclosed, which will help trap the scent where it can be enjoyed.

If you're shopping for old-fashioned favorites like roses or sweet peas, keep in mind that many newer cultivars are bred to be tougher than their ancestors. While

The light apple scent of 'Apple Blossom' climbing rose (*Rosa* 'Apple Blossom') is deliciously sweet, but also subtle.

this means blooms that are potentially longer lasting or more dramatic, as well as offering longer vase life for cut flowers, oftentimes the trade-off for enhanced performance is muting of a plant's signature scent. In roses, for instance, the gene that carries disease resistance is unfortunately not compatible with the gene for fragrance. Select retailers, many online, do carry strongly scented rose varieties that also resist disease and are long bloomers. David Austin produces several, including 'Gertrude Jekyll', 'Ambridge Rose', and 'Lady Emma Hamilton'. Similarly, heirloom varieties of sweet peas (*Lathyrus odoratus*) brought into cultivation in the seventeenth and eighteenth centuries – such as 'Cupani' or 'Painted Lady', that must be planted from seed – generally bear more fragrant blooms than ones purchased at the nursery. Because of this, if you are growing a flower specifically to enjoy its perfume, you might need to look a little farther than your local garden center or big box store to find a worthy cultivar.

above If you enjoy your garden in the evening, consider plants that release their fragrance at night, such as evening stock (*Matthiola incana*).

right Not all garden scents need to be flowery. Pineapple sage (*Salvia elegans*) emits a fruity aroma reminiscent of pineapple.

We're all familiar with the expression "stop and smell the roses," and a garden's ability to encourage us to slow down and drink in its sights and scents is one of its most powerful gifts. A scent doesn't have to be bold to be enjoyable. Making the extra effort to seek out the source of an elusive scent can make the experience of walking through a garden that much more rewarding. Think of scent as another layer to your garden—happily, one that doesn't require a lot of space or energy!

If traditional flowery scents don't appeal to you, remember that many plants have subtle fragrances more reminiscent of a well-stocked kitchen pantry than a department store perfume counter. The flowers of the azara tree (*Azara macrophylla*) and fiveleaf akebia vine (*Akebia quinata*) are often described as smelling lightly of chocolate, while both Joe Pye weed (*Eutrochium purpureum*) and sweet almond verbena shrub (*Aloysia virgata*) exude a light vanilla scent. If you prefer a fruitier aroma, opt for the ripe notes of pineapple sage (*Salvia elegans*) or the tangy fragrance of lemon verbena (*Aloysia citrodora*).

Beyond flowers, herbs are an outstanding way to add another layer of fragrance to the garden. Salvias and sages are culinary and ornamental herbs that make wonderful garden additions because their spicy, bracing aromas are unique to the outdoors. Unlike many flowers, which send their fragrance out into the atmosphere on their own, you must interact with an herb to release its scent. Because the scent is typically held in the foliage as well as the flowers, brushing your hand along a leaf-covered stem will lightly bruise the leaves, allowing its bracing fragrance to escape. Another option is to plant small patches of aromatic ground covers close to pathways or between paving stones. Creeping thyme, chamomile, and golden culinary sage will release subtle fragrances when stepped on. Why pay a premium for calming lavender-scented aromatherapy products when you could simply step outside and run your hands along your own marvelous plant?

Scent plays an important role in mood, memory, and emotion.

hardscape elements

For most of us, the word garden brings plants to mind, but in fact, the non-living elements in your garden are equally important to how the whole space looks and feels. Hardscape in the form of patios, decks, pathways, walls, and other constructs create the strong lines and shapes that help define a garden's character. In modest-sized lots, hardscape takes on a particularly important role, as it often makes up anywhere from 25 to 75 percent of the finished landscape. You might be surprised to know that when I am designing a backyard landscape, only about a quarter of my time is spent choosing and siting plants. The rest goes toward laying out the footprint and determining other important features, including hardscape — in other words, all the man-made elements in a landscape. Of all the various types of hardscape a backyard can include, the patio or deck is typically the most important. Not only is it the place you are most likely spend the majority of your outdoor time, it often serves as both a visual and physical transition from the indoors to outside. Just as the kitchen is the heart of the home, the patio is the center of the backyard.

Pavers and brick combine for a rustic effect appropriate for this informal garden.

Choosing Materials

Deciding on the right materials for your patio or deck is an important part of the design process. There are several factors to consider, the first of which is aesthetics. Should the space feel casual or formal? Rustic or sophisticated? Your personal taste will be an important guiding factor when designing your yard. If you love the crispness of concrete and shy away from the loose feel of gravel, for example, then you are already moving toward a modern treatment. Beyond likes and dislikes, however, it is a good idea to consider how any materials you choose will fit with your property as a whole, including the front yard, the architecture, and perhaps even your home's interior. Avoid thinking of hardscape as a stand-alone decision and instead treat it as part of a bigger picture.

Taking inspiration from the existing features of your home's architecture is the most logical and intuitive place to start. Take a look at the materials and colors on the house's exterior. If your home is partially faced with a decorative finish, such as a brick or stone border along the lower half of the building, choosing a similar treatment would tie the two together. It may not be practical or desirable to use the exact material, but selecting paving or wood for a deck in the same color family will still make the house feel connected to the outdoor spaces. In smaller gardens, when choosing hardscape materials, a balance should be struck. On one hand, adding too many disparate materials can clutter up a yard, but conversely, too *much* repetition can lead to monotony. An all-brick house with an all-brick patio, for example, would be a bit much visually. To make the two relate without looking too monotonous, treat the reference material as a detail or accent, rather than a stand-alone element. If your house is sided in brick, for example, consider using colored concrete or bluestone as the primary material for the hardscape, then accent it with a brick border.

Similar materials are not the only way to keep the landscape integrated. Choosing patio materials that stay within the same color family as the house will also connect the two. Mediterranean-style homes with stucco roofs and tile accents, houses made of brick or stone, and those painted in shades of gold, beige, or brown tend to look best with materials that reflect their warmth. Many flagstones, including Arizona flagstone, are available in this color profile, as well as brick, gravel, colored concrete, and, in warmer climates, ceramic or Saltillo tile.

Homes that are either painted or constructed with materials in shades of gray, blue, or green are best complemented by hardscape dominated by similar cool colors. Cobblestone pavers, bluestone flagstone, and blue-toned brick are choices to consider. Wood, particularly if stained a darker color, makes a particularly rich choice. When working with this color family, I prefer to stay away from all but the lightest concretes, and avoid gravel or gray-toned decomposed granite, as these tend to result in a commercial feel unsuited to residential gardens.

Consider whether your home's style is formal or informal, and match the hardscape in temperament. The charm of a bungalow or ranch house suggests a different

The warm tones of the home's stucco walls are repeated in the stacked stone, flagstone, and tile used in the landscape.

approach to hardscape than the elegance of a Georgian or Greek revival residence, for example. Although most materials can work well with either style, the colors, forms, and how the materials are combined determine their success. In general, flagstones or pavers that are smooth and are laid in a geometric pattern suggest more formality, while irregularly shaped flagstone, more roughly finished cobblestone-style pavers, or thickly cut stones create a more relaxed impression. Flagstone, brick, or pavers that are mortared down also tend to feel more formal than when they are dry laid onto a bed of compacted gravel and their joints filled with sand, gravel, or ground cover.

Keep budget in mind when you think about hardscape as well. In general, anything that is mortared onto a concrete pad (flagstone, tile, or some brick) will be more expensive than when those materials are dry laid. Even if your design falls easily

The color of this patio's pavers mimics the warmth of the home's brick exterior.

within your budget, remember that it is still important to take your time choosing materials. Changing your mind about a plant and swapping it out with another is one thing. Addressing a hardscape mistake is likely to be much costlier.

A key tenet of the less is more approach to garden design is creating a yard where less is time spent on upkeep and more is time spent relaxing. For that reason, maintenance requirements are as important to consider as aesthetics. Some materials will require regular cleaning, sealing, or staining. Durability is also an issue, as this affects not only appearance, but also how soon a patio will need to be replaced or repaired. And finally, think about how the rest of the garden might affect a material's suitability. Is it in full sun in a spot where bare feet are the norm? If so, stick to more reflective colors to keep things as cool as possible. Will nearby plants increase your maintenance chores? Flowering or deciduous trees that drop a lot of litter won't work well with gravel or jointed pavers that are difficult to clean.

Investigating the durability, cost, and ongoing maintenance requirements of some of the most in-demand hardscape materials can help you decide which is best for you. The following brief overview of some of the more popular choices can help you narrow your selection, but it is a good idea to do additional research before making a final decision, particularly as regional differences can greatly affect pricing and maintenance. All of these materials are appropriate for modest-sized yards.

Avoid locating gravel patios near trees like ornamental pear (*Pyrus calleryana*). Its excessive flower bud litter is too small to be easily raked.

opposite Wood is an attractive and durable choice in multi-level gardens.

Wood and wood composites

If your backyard's most usable space isn't right outside the door, a deck might be a more practical choice than multiple sets of stairs that angle down to a patio. Wood makes an excellent choice as it is soft and easy to shape and unlike most materials that would simply break, wood under light stress will flex and return to its original shape. The durability of a wood deck is directly related to the species chosen for it. Different woods are popular in different parts of the country, but a general rule of thumb is to stick to harder woods like cedar and redwood. Be aware that there are also different grades of the same wood, and even different categories within individual species, depending on the intended application. The strongest wood is from the inner portion of the tree, which becomes very dense and hard over time. That means redwood that is graded Construction Heart, for example, will be more expensive but also more resistant to insect problems and decay than B Grade, which comes from the outer layer of the tree. Beyond these traditional choices, tropical hardwoods such as ipe are becoming increasingly popular with homeowners. Among the most durable woods available, tropical species create decks that are strong and stable in virtually any environment. Ipe is durable and attractive, but its density makes installation more complex, which can result in a high price tag. If you are considering this as an option, it is worth seeking out an experienced installer and reputable lumber source.

Wood decks do require regular maintenance to prevent warping and/or fading. To maximize both looks and longevity, wood decks should be cleaned and sealed

Less maintenance and upkeep makes plastic composite decking a potential alternative to traditional wood.

annually. This is generally a multi-day process, and should be done in late spring. Preparation consists of sweeping the deck clear of debris (which may require cleaning crevices with a putty knife) followed by either scrubbing or pressure washing the entire surface. If necessary, lightly sand and make any minor repairs. At this point, the wood is ready to seal or re-stain.

By contrast, composite decking, which goes by various manufactured names like Trex or TimberTech, requires less maintenance. A plastic composite deck is generally more expensive to install, but this is counterbalanced by the reduced cost and commitment compared to wood. An annual pressure washing is generally all that's required. This makes it a popular choice for those who want to minimize garden chores. The look of plastic composite is generally considered less attractive than the rich, natural appearance of hardwood. While its durability and ease of maintenance are appealing qualities, composite decking may weather unevenly, if part of it is in shade and part is in sun. It can also become scratched from pets or heavy usage. Unlike a wood deck, sanding and staining can't address blemishes like these, although some brands offer upgrades like UV protection and scratch-resistant coatings.

Note that when decks are located in shade in areas of the country with relatively high humidity, moss growth on both wood and composite decking can be a problem. It is generally easier to clean a composite deck than one made from wood, as a power washer (and tri-sodium phosphate if needed) are all that is required.

Flagstone

Flagstone is an excellent choice for patios because of its natural beauty, durability, and range of color options. Many of the most popular types of flagstone for patios, such as bluestone, limestone, and Arizona sandstone, vary considerably in cost and durability. Arizona sandstone is usually less expensive than other options, but it is also more porous, making it more likely to break or stain over time. For that reason, it is not always the best choice for a high-traffic area, or where cooking or tree litter can lead to staining. Harder stones, such as bluestone or granite, are more expensive initially, but their longevity can make them a better value over the long run.

Flagstone is often installed in a free-form or irregular pattern, and can be either mortared onto a concrete pad or dry laid over a bed of compacted gravel. With dry-laid patios, the joints are filled with sand, gravel, or ground cover. In warm climates, the increased stability and cleanliness of a mortared patio make it a good option for a primary patio or one that gets a lot of use. Dry-laid patios work better farther away from the house, where loose joint sand and ground cover debris are less likely to be tracked indoors. Although flagstone properly installed over a compacted subbase will be quite stable, the natural movement of soil often causes the stones to become uneven over time.

Conversely, dry laying is the most popular method of installation in colder climates. Because freeze and thaw cycles can make it difficult for stone to adhere to the concrete, a bonding agent must be used for a mortared patio in a cold climate. The freeze and thaw cycle also means joint mortar is more prone to cracking over time, and it is often difficult to exactly match the existing mortar color when repairs are made. Dry-laid patios tend to be more forgiving of any heaving and falling of the subsoil, and if they do become uneven, are easier to repair.

A mortared flagstone patio is also one of the most expensive hardscape options; you're paying for the beauty of natural stone and for durability. Even if a low-cost stone is chosen, the expense comes in laying the concrete pad and installing and mortaring the stone—a multistep process requiring professional labor. Irregular-cut patios are generally the most expensive of all, as trying to fit random shapes into a defined area generates a certain amount of waste and requires skill to install in an aesthetically pleasing way. By contrast, a dry-laid patio is less expensive to install and, with the proper equipment and planning, can even be a DIY project.

Bluestone laid in a random pattern with right angles (right) has a more formal appearance than when laid in a free-form or irregular pattern (left).

A free-form dry-laid patio
with ground cover between
its joints requires more effort
to maintain than one with
mortared joints.

Mortared flagstone patios are relatively low-maintenance options. Sealing them annually will help retain color and discourage staining, but depending on the stone you choose, this may not be necessary. Otherwise, an occasional scrubbing or pressure washing is all that is required. In contrast, a dry-laid patio's joint material will require maintenance. Whatever joint medium you choose needs some level of regular attention, whether it's keeping ground covers healthy and trimmed back from the stones, or periodically refreshing sand or gravel levels. Over time, if a dry-laid patio becomes too uneven, portions may need to be pulled up and re-installed.

Flagstone comes in a range of thicknesses. Thinner cuts are more economical and preferred for mortared applications, but search out flagstone that is at least 1.5 to 2 inches thick to discourage movement and make a dry-laid patio more stable. Most joint compounds will settle and compact over time, leaving gaps that are unsightly and can be tripping hazards. Unless drainage is expected to be an issue, plan to space your stones as close together as possible; tighter joints create a cleaner, more polished look and result in less upkeep. Aim for joints between .5 and 2 inches.

Pavers

The word "pavers" is an umbrella term that refers to a range of man-made patio stones. They are usually rectangular, square, or designed to fit in interlocking patterns. A patio made from these materials generally has a mortared perimeter (often referred to as a soldier course), while the interior of the space is made from tightly placed bricks over a compacted subbase. The two most common are brick pavers, made from clay, and concrete pavers, which are often referred to as cobblestone pavers because they are designed to be reminiscent of their historic precedents.

The warm, traditional look of brick makes for a timeless choice that never goes out of style. Brick pavers are highly durable and, while they can become cracked or broken over time, will generally last for many years. They are stain resistant and less prone to fading than concrete pavers, so they do not require sealing; this makes them a particularly low-maintenance option.

Concrete pavers are made by compressing concrete and aggregate into preformed molds. Because of this, they come in a wide variety of colors and sizes. They vary in price depending on style and manufacturer, but they are generally less expensive than brick,

dry-laid patio tips

You can simply dig a shallow bed and lay flagstone directly on the ground, but your patio will be much more stable over the long haul if it is built over a properly compacted subbase of drainage rock or sand. The depth of any subbase materials and whether or not drainage piping should be added is dependent on the permeability of the native soil. Heavier clay soils often require a deeper base and additional drainage.

Rustic pavers are a low-maintenance choice for casual spaces.

previous page Brick patios can easily take on a formal or informal tone.

both to purchase and install. Since they tend to be more precisely cut than brick, concrete pavers can be easier for DIYers to work with. In contrast to brick, the pigment used to color the cement in concrete pavers is vulnerable to UV rays and will fade over time, making the stone and sand that forms the aggregate more prominent. For this reason, regular sealing is recommended.

Concrete

Concrete is fast becoming the most popular patio material in many parts of the country, for a number of reasons: it's less labor intensive than most other patio materials to install, it is reasonably priced, and it can easily be formed into a range of decorative options, making it appropriate for a variety of design styles. Stamping, dyeing, and staining can also elevate the aesthetic impact of concrete far above utilitarian plain gray. With its contemporary look, however, concrete is not always a good choice for more historied parts of the country, such as the coastal Northeast.

While concrete is generally very durable, it can stain, so regular sealing is recommended though not required. More important, it is prone to cracking and heaving over time. This is particularly true in areas where the ground shifts dramatically in response to climates with regular freeze-thaw cycles or on properties with a high water table. Planting a large tree with surface roots close to a concrete patio can also wreak havoc. While there is no way to completely protect against cracking, the visual impact of any fine cracks that eventually develop can be minimized by choosing a stamped pattern that mimics the slightly uneven surface of slate or flagstone.

One caveat when selecting a stamp option: while replicating the uneven surface of natural stone creates an attractive finished look, for the best look, I advise avoiding stamps that try to mimic the irregular shape of natural stone or pavers, as the artificial joint lines embedded in the stamp pattern look like poor imitations of the real thing. Beyond that, in order to minimize cracking, score lines must be superimposed at intervals over the stamped pattern on the patio, creating competing lines that make it look even more unnatural. A better option is to use what is sometimes referred to as a slate-skin stamp, which mimics the natural, uneven finish of stone, but without outlining the borders of each "stone" in an artificial way. If score lines are a necessity, use them as an opportunity to create a pattern that enhances the patio's dimensions or delineates spaces. A diagonal pattern spaced at 5- or 6-foot intervals will give the patio a sharp, finished look evocative of oversized stones. It is better to have a patio made of great-looking concrete than one that looks like it is trying to emulate more expensive materials.

A slate-skin concrete stamp designed to mimic the rough finish of slate—but without imitation stone outlines—can be finished with diagonal score lines spaced 5 feet apart.

Gravel

Gravel can create a lovely casual surface for a garden space, and works equally well in traditional and contemporary gardens. Its informality lends itself to intimate spaces, making this a particularly attractive choice for smaller gardens. It also pairs well with naturalistic landscapes, while its organic nature can soften the rigid geometry that's often a part of modern designs. As well, gravel is one of the least expensive paving options available, and requires less subbase preparation than most other hardscape materials. Installation costs are modest. In general, opt for gravel in warm tones, often marketed with names like California Gold or Yellow Marble. Be cautious with cool shades of blue and gray, which tend to look more like base rock than finished gravel in home gardens.

After aesthetics, take practical considerations into account, like whether the stone will feel comfortable underfoot—it's counterintuitive, but angular stone compacts more efficiently and therefore makes for a more stable walking surface. Similarly, it is much more challenging to scoot chairs in and out around a dining table on a gravel patio than a hard surface.

Gravel gardens also require regular maintenance, a key consideration for those who want to keep chores to the barest minimum. Any leaf litter or debris from nearby trees or shrubs—not to mention excess soil or mulch from the surrounding plants—will readily mix in with the gravel and be quite difficult to remove, creating a messy appearance. Raking gravel monthly keeps things tidy. Gravel also must be

A concrete patio with a stamped finish is an attractive and low-maintenance hardscape option.

opposite Gravel patios contrast beautifully with adjacent planting beds, and have a softer effect than many other hardscape choices.

refreshed periodically, a maintenance expense to consider. In areas with winter snow that must be shoveled or plowed regularly, gravel inevitably winds up where it's not supposed to be, requiring additional annual clean up in surrounding lawns and garden beds. For all these reasons, I avoid using gravel for primary recreation areas, and instead prefer to use it as a ground cover material for smaller, secondary patios away from any overhead trees or large shrubbery.

beautiful, low-maintenance plants

Selecting plants is one of the most rewarding parts of designing a new garden or refreshing an existing one, but it can also be one of the most stressful. So many plants to choose from! This is especially challenging when your space is limited. A tour through the local garden center can sound like a relaxing way to spend an hour or two — until you realize you're not certain whether the plants you admire will get too big or stay too small, bloom at the time of year you want them to, or need more maintenance than you are willing to provide.

Brightly colored and boldly textured foliage make this Florida garden a standout.

Earth-toned 'Bronze Baby' New Zealand flax (*Phormium tenax* 'Bronze Baby') and chartreuse Japanese forest grass (*Hakonechloa macra* 'Aureola') contrast richly against a bright green ground cover.

I was a new gardener in my twenties when my husband and I purchased our first home. I recall how excited I was to go to the nursery and choose plants to fill a border in the backyard. I spent a happy afternoon planting a cheerful flower bed in a riot of colors and couldn't wait to show it off to my mother, a long-time gardener whom I was certain would be impressed by my first serious attempt at gardening. Imagine my disappointment when, a few weeks later, all the flowers were spent! Expecting a summer's worth of blooms, I hadn't realized that the pansies, ranunculus, and delphiniums I had chosen were only destined to shine for a short time.

While gardening newbies can be forgiven for filling an entire border with short-term bloomers, even experienced gardeners can unintentionally create a garden that shines only briefly, or requires more time and maintenance than is practical. Appealing though it may be to toss plants in your cart that catch your fancy, your garden will be much more successful in the long run if you arrive for plant buying armed with a basic game plan. Begin by focusing on the plants that will make up the foundation of your small garden, then treat flowering perennials or annuals as icing on the cake.

Shrubs as Foundation Plants

Shrubs add beauty without excessive upkeep. Although there are exceptions, shrubs are generally less maintenance-intensive than other types of plants. Unlike trees, they typically don't require professional pruning. They live longer than perennials and of course annuals, which must be replanted every year. Not all shrubs are created equal, however, so it is worth seeking out ones that will maximize the look of your less is more landscape while keeping garden chores in check.

Because it's common to choose plants and install them in warmer months, it is important to understand that a lush summer garden can look substantially different in winter—especially if you choose too many deciduous shrubs, which lose their leaves in cold weather. While there is no strict design guideline, I recommend aiming for a backyard that is between 50 and 80 percent evergreen. If the ratio is lower than that, your garden will feel too bare in winter. This applies to colder climates as well, as evergreen plants provide structure even when covered in snow. Rely on deciduous, flowering shrubs and perennials to add seasonal interest.

Keep in mind that evergreen simply means a plant won't lose its leaves in cold weather. It doesn't mean you need to stick exclusively to green foliage, as a garden filled with nothing but variations of green can be a bit tedious. To maximize impact in a small space with the least amount of maintenance, look for evergreen plants in a range of foliage colors and textures. A garden whose shades of green are punctuated by contrasting reds or burgundies, elegant silvers, or cheerful chartreuses will look attractive all year round, even when nothing is blooming.

A variety of textures will also add depth and complexity to your shrub palette. Complement the small- to medium-sized leaves of workhorse shrubs like boxwood (*Buxus sempervirens*) and Indian hawthorn (*Rhaphiolepis indica*) with plants whose foliage displays contrasting textures, such as the broad, oversized leaves of hostas and cannas or the elongated leaves of cordylines and ornamental grasses. Choosing low-maintenance plants with a mix of leaf colors and textures is a key designer strategy for creating a backyard garden that shines in any season with a minimum of care.

The bluish tint in the leaves of hens and chicks (*Echeveria ×imbricata*) is echoed in the blue stripe of nearby 'Gold Strike' lily-of-the-Nile (*Agapanthus* 'Gold Strike').

plants with colorful foliage

Striking leaf color and manageable size make these excellent choices for establishing the foundation for a modest-sized garden.

Shrub or Perennial	USDA zones	Foliage description
'Kaleidoscope' abelia (*Abelia* × *grandiflora* 'Kaleidoscope')	6–9	Foliage color varies throughout the year. New spring growth is a mix of bright yellow and lime green, gradually deepening to golden yellow. Autumn and winter bring shades of red and orange. 3 to 5 feet high and wide.
'Blue Glow' agave (*Agave* 'Blue Glow')	6–10	Stiff blue foliage is banded by narrow red margins that glow subtly when touched by sunlight. 2 to 3 feet high and wide.
PLATINUM BEAUTY mat rush (*Lomandra longifolia* 'Roma 13' PP25962)	8–10	Tough, grass-like perennial with evergreen foliage. Elegant variegated leaves add movement to the garden. Tolerant of heat and drought, this plant lends a touch of elegance to low-water gardens. 2 to 3 feet high and wide.
'Diablo' ninebark (*Physocarpus opulifolius* 'Diablo')	2–9	Dense burgundy leaves make this shrub a standout. With creamy white flowers in summer, this plant's scale makes it a lovely companion for larger ornamental grasses in shades of chartreuse and silver.
'Meerlo' lavender (*Lavandula allardii* 'Meerlo')	9–10	Frilly leaves strikingly striped in shades of creamy yellow and soft blue. A stunning companion for blue-foliaged succulents such as agave or hens and chicks (*Echeveria* ×*imbricata*), which echo the blue-green leaves. 2 to 3 feet high and 2 to 4 feet wide.
'Tequila Sunrise' mirror plant (*Coprosma* 'Tequila Sunrise')	9–10	New green leaves with gold margins emerge in spring, gradually morphing into rusty orange and red. Cold weather brings brilliantly colored foliage in bright reds and oranges. 2 to 5 feet high and 2 to 4 feet wide.

clockwise, from top left
'Kaleidoscope' abelia, 'Blue Glow' agave, 'Diablo' ninebark, 'Tequila Sunrise' mirror plant, 'Meerlo' lavender, PLATINUM BEAUTY mat rush

dwarf versions of popular shrubs

For many, pruning is one of the most stressful garden chores, as knowing when and how to prune each garden plant requires more expertise than casual gardeners aspire to. This is especially true in modest-sized yards, where many readily available shrubs can outgrow their space in just a few years. To avoid having to prune shrubs to a desired size, choose appropriately sized plants for your space from the get-go. If you plant a hedge with shrubs that will ultimately grow 10 feet around with the intention of maintaining them at 4 feet, expect to be trimming your plants throughout the year. Not only is this a tedious chore, but keeping plants smaller than their natural size means they frequently get pruned or "poodled" into unnatural shapes. Because this process regularly removes new growth, flowers will also be minimized and the bare branches in the plants' interiors will gradually become more exposed. "Right plant, right place" is an axiom of responsible gardening—less pruning means less waste to haul away to the landfill or compost heap. The plants recommended here retain their small stature and should require only occasional light pruning to keep their shape.

Shrub	USDA zones	Description
'Little John' dwarf bottlebrush (*Callistemon viminalis* 'Little John')	9–10	A low-growing evergreen shrub that fits perfectly into a sunny, low-water spot. Brilliant red flowers are attractive to pollinators. 2 to 5 feet high and 3 to 5 feet wide.
PETITE PLUM butterfly bush (*Buddleia davidii* PETITE PLUM)	5–9	This dwarf, deciduous version of butterfly bush boasts a tidy, compact habit that requires little care other than an annual pruning in early spring. 3 to 6 feet high and wide.
DEAR DOLORES hydrangea (*Hydrangea macrophylla* DEAR DOLORES)	5–9	A compact cultivar that reaches only 4 to 5 feet high and wide. Its generous, blue flowers are perfect to light up a shady spot. A strong spring bloomer that reblooms summer to fall.

Shrub	USDA zones	Description
'Little Kiss' sage (*Salvia microphylla* 'Little Kiss')	8–9	Red-and-white flowers bloom over a long season like popular 'Hot Lips' sage, but the compact habit of 'Little Kiss' makes it more suited to smaller gardens. 18 inches high and wide.
BLUE GEM coast rosemary (*Westringia* BLUE GEM)	9–11	Australian evergreen BLUE GEM coast rosemary has prolific blooms and delicate foliage. Takes well to pruning if a smaller size is preferred. 4 to 6 feet high and 3 to 5 feet wide.
dwarf myrtle (*Myrtus communis* 'Compacta')	9–11	An excellent choice for adding year-round structure to sunny gardens. Requires little pruning, but is easy to shear into a low hedge for a more formal look. 3 to 4 feet high and wide.

clockwise, from top left 'Little John' dwarf bottle-brush, PETITE PLUM butterfly bush, DEAR DOLORES hydrangea, dwarf myrtle, BLUE GEM coast rosemary, 'Hot Lips' sage—very similar to smaller 'Little Kiss'

a word about roses in small spaces

A dedicated rose garden might not be the best approach for homeowners with limited space. Most traditional roses require plentiful air circulation to stay healthy, which means leaving large spaces between plants. Average-sized and smaller lots are generally more attractive when densely planted. Furthermore, when arranged in a formal or traditional style, rose bushes are usually chosen for their individual qualities, resulting in a range of flower colors not necessarily intended to harmonize—this can create a chaotic effect in a small backyard.

A better strategy is to choose roses with cultural attributes and flower color that can be attractively incorporated into the yard, rather than being segregated in a designated quadrant. FLOWER CARPET and KNOCK OUT roses are bred to be disease resistant and mostly trouble-free. Many will also bloom over a longer season than traditional roses, an asset in a smaller space where all plants need to pull their weight. When choosing any rose, it is worth reading tags carefully to understand disease resistance and bloom season to ensure you are getting a long-flowering, standout performer. I am partial to 'Betty Boop' (*Rosa* 'Betty Boop'), for its prolific bloom and resistance to disease. New flowers emerge with rich pink edges and yellow throats, fading to a soft ivory with pale pink margins as the flowers mature. In my own garden, an annual application of compost and a hard pruning in late winter are all the care this superstar rose requires to look its best.

Easy care roses like 'Amber' (*Rosa* FLOWER CARPET 'Amber') are good choices for smaller gardens as they stay compact and mix easily in the landscape.

'Betty Boop' rose (*Rosa* 'Betty Boop') is non-fussy, disease resistant, and blooms over a long season.

Redefining a Four-Season Garden

Laying down an evergreen, foliage-centric foundation is the easiest way to ensure a backyard that looks great all year with a minimum of maintenance. If this becomes your entire planting strategy, however, you are missing out on one of gardening's great pleasures: watching the way plants reflect the seasons. We all live lives that are in tune with seasonal changes, whether it's the start of the school year in September or the celebration of summer on July Fourth. Plants can help deepen our enjoyment of the uniqueness of each time of year. And unlike the effort it takes to decorate for the holidays or live up to your New Year's resolutions, with some simple planning, your garden will welcome each season with minimal intervention from you.

The phrase "four-season garden" can be a little confusing, as it may conjure up an image of a backyard bursting with blooms and color every month of the year. For most of us, though, it isn't practical to devote major space to one-season plants that will not contribute in a meaningful way the rest of the year. Include one or two superstars that reflect each of the four seasons instead, and you'll always have something special to enjoy — and to look forward to.

Spring

Spring is the season of anticipation, as the garden slowly awakens and begins to bloom again. This is especially true in colder parts of the country. One dramatic tree or shrub with blooms that cover every branch conveys the exuberance we feel as warmer days approach. I am particularly fond of plants whose flowers appear before the leaves unfurl, offering a brilliant, monochromatic color effect; there is nothing cheerier to brighten up a dark, dismal day and remind you that spring has arrived than the sight of an ornamental pear or cherry in all its flower-covered glory. Because it's often too cool in early spring to enjoy extended time outdoors, I urge my clients to place a spring superstar in a spot where it can be viewed from a much-used room, like the family room or kitchen.

Summer

In many ways, summer is the easiest time of year to showcase a garden; so many flowering perennials are at their best then. This is also the season of backyard barbecues and dinners on the patio, so making sure the garden looks attractive is often a priority. As tempting as plants are that boast beautiful flowers, avoid any that bloom for only three or four weeks; a better strategy is to plant those that will go all season — and then some.

For example, many of my clients request lavender (*Lavandula* spp.) for their gardens. It handles the heat and drought common in Northern California and is

right Delicate columbine (*Aquilegia* spp.) is a welcome spring bloomer.

far right A rustic grape arbor ushers visitors into a garden filled with summer blooms.

Ornamental grasses mixed with dark purple houseleek (*Aeonium arboreum* 'Zwartkop') make a charming autumn combination.

attractive and fragrant. On the downside, however, many varieties have an initial rush of blooms that look great for four or five weeks, but then bloom only sporadically for the rest of the summer. In comparison, catmint (*Nepeta* spp.) begins blooming in spring and, in mild climates, will keep producing flowers until first frost. A simple haircut midsummer when flowers are spent will result in a second or often third round of blooms.

In winter, this garden takes on a sculptural quality.

Autumn

Spring and summer are all about showy flowers, but a subtler form of beauty characterizes fall. As days grow shorter and the sun sits lower in the sky, the quality of light becomes more luminous. Incorporating a few ornamental grasses in your plant palette is a wonderful way to help you appreciate autumn's softer light. Sometimes referred to as light catchers, the long, delicate flowers of most ornamental grasses seem to glow when kissed by the sun. Early morning and late afternoon, when the sun provides dramatic backlighting, are particularly good times to admire elegant plumes and seed heads.

Winter

Winter may be the season least associated with active gardening. Perennials die back, trees lose their leaves, and most plants settle into a phase of restful dormancy. Yet this quieter, starker beauty has a special appeal, as it allows us to appreciate plants' underlying forms. The painter Andrew Wyeth was not alone in feeling this way when he wrote, "I prefer winter and fall, when you feel the bone structure in the landscape."

While winter encourages us to admire the architecture of most deciduous plants, not all plants shut down for the season. To complement the calm of a cold-season garden, choose one or two plants whose colorful show of berries or blooms or intoxicating scent will liven up the landscape in the darker months.

spring standouts

Spring is a time of new beginnings, and trees or shrubs that put on a spectacular display of blooms just as winter winds to a close are the perfect way to usher in the season.

Tree or shrub	USDA zones	Description
'Paul's Scarlet' hawthorn (*Crataegus laevigata* 'Paul's Scarlet')	5–9	In spring, dark pink blossoms cover the branches. Pinkish red berries persist into winter, providing some cold-season interest as well as acting as a food source for foraging birds.
flowering dogwood (*Cornus florida* spp.)	5–9	Flowering dogwood puts on a spectacular early spring show. Blooms consist of four ivory-colored bracts containing a cluster of tiny yellow flowers.
ornamental crabapple (*Malus* spp.)	3–8	Perfect for a lavish spring display, with a color spectrum of blooms ranging from white to blush to deeper shades of pink and red.
Chinese fringe tree (*Chionanthus retusus*)	3–9	Delicate, lightly scented flowers fall in clusters like fringe on a shawl. A particularly graceful addition to a springtime garden.
WINE AND ROSES weigela (*Weigela florida* 'Alexandra' WINE AND ROSES)	5–9	Dark velvety leaves and striking pink blossoms deliver a one-two springtime punch. Masses of vivid pink flowers bloom over a long season beginning in April, followed by a second bloom in late summer.
'Purple Pony' purple leaf plum (*Prunus cerasifera* 'Purple Pony')	4–9	A natural dwarf that seldom grows more than 12 feet tall—excellent for small-space gardeners. Single, shell-pink blooms cover the tree in early to midspring, and are followed by rich purple foliage.

clockwise, from top left
'Paul's Scarlet' hawthorn, flowering dogwood, Chinese fringe tree, 'Purple Pony' purple leaf plum, WINE AND ROSES weigela, ornamental crabapple

long-blooming summer perennials

The long, lazy days of summer are best enjoyed from a shady spot—not out in the garden planting annuals or deadheading. To get the longest bloom for the least effort, opt for perennials that reward with flowers all through the hottest months.

Summer perennials	USDA zones	Description
blackfoot daisy (*Melampodium leucanthum*)	7–9	Small, white, daisy-like flowers that begin blooming in spring and continue through summer. If plants get leggy, a trim keeps them flowering into the fall.
'Early Sunrise' tickseed (*Coreopsis grandiflora* 'Early Sunrise')	4–9	Bright yellow flowers that bloom on and off, spring through early fall. Extremely tough, thriving in a variety of soils and conditions.
FIREWITCH garden pinks (*Dianthus* 'Feuerhexe' FIREWITCH)	3–9	Deliciously scented rose-pink flowers begin blooming in late spring and continue through summer. More drought tolerant than other garden pinks, making FIREWITCH a good choice for hot, dry gardens.
'Illumination Apricot' digiplexis (*Digiplexis* 'Illumination Apricot')	8–9	This non-stop bloomer keeps going from spring into early fall. Spikes of blooms up to 3 feet tall hold rich pink flowers with apricot throats above rich green foliage.
hyssop (*Agastache* spp.)	5–9	Fragrant, tubular flowers appear along stems, lasting through summer and attracting pollinators. Available in a wide range of flower colors, this drought-tolerant plant requires little maintenance.
coleus (*Solenostemon scutellarioides*)	All	Although not a perennial, coleus is one of the few annuals worth the effort to replant each year. Its vibrant-colored leaves make it impactful in semi-shady areas. Pale blue or white flower spikes appear in late summer.

clockwise, from top left
blackfoot daisy, 'Early Sunrise' tickseed, 'Illumination Apricot' digiplexis, hyssop, coleus, FIREWITCH garden pinks

movement and light for autumn

With their gauzy sprays of flowers and delicate stems that shiver with the slightest hint of wind, ornamental grasses are the perfect plants to capture the warm light and soft breezes of autumn.

Autumn beauties	USDA zones	Description
ruby grass (*Melinis nerviglumis*)	9–10	Forms a 2-foot clump of blue-green foliage, which turns purplish red as the weather grows colder. Showy pink flowers persist into fall. 2 feet high and wide.
'Little Zebra' dwarf zebra grass (*Miscanthus sinensis* 'Little Zebra')	5–9	Graceful, lemony green leaves with pale yellow stripes make a dramatic statement. In late summer, ivory plumes tinged with purple rise above the foliage. 3 to 4 feet high and wide.
pink muhly grass (*Muhlenbergia capillaris*)	7–9	Outstanding medium-sized grass that puts up dramatic sprays of puffy pink flowers in autumn. 3 to 4 feet high and wide.
oriental fountain grass (*Pennisetum orientale*)	5–9	Forms a gently arching mound of delicate green foliage. Straw-colored flower stalks arch gracefully above the leaves and persist into autumn, adding color and movement. 2 to 4 feet high and wide.
orange sedge (*Carex testacea*)	5–9	An evergreen that shifts color throughout the year, from bronzy, forest green to bright orange under the right conditions. 1 foot high by 2 to 3 feet wide.
variegated reed grass (*Calamagrostis* × *acutiflora*)	5–9	The same fountain-like base of narrow, arching leaves and tall spikes of wheat-colored flowers as popular 'Karl Forester' feather reed grass, but with variegated foliage and in a more petite form. 2 to 3 feet tall and wide. 3- to 4-foot flower spikes in summer and fall.

clockwise, from top left
ruby grass, 'Little Zebra'
dwarf zebra grass, oriental
fountain grass, variegated
reed grass, orange sedge,
pink muhly grass

blooms, berries, and scent for winter

There's no need to let your entire garden go dormant when winter rolls around. By choosing one or two trees or shrubs that put on their prettiest faces in cold weather, you'll ensure your garden has a cheerful counterpoint to the season's dampness and cold.

Winter Stunners	USDA zones	Description
Darwin's barberry (*Berberis darwinii*)	7–9	In early winter, tangerine buds tinged with red appear on this evergreen version of barberry, followed by vibrant orange blooms in late winter. If space is an issue, choose a dwarf version such as 'Carolina Compacta' or 'Nana'.
saucer magnolia (*Magnolia × soulan-geana* spp.)	4–9	Flowers in shades of white and pink appear before new leaves emerge, making this tree a cold-season showstopper. Cultivars such as 'San Jose' and 'Alba' begin flowering in winter. The 'Little Girl' series offers a good selection of smaller specimens.
scarlet firethorn (*Pyracantha coccinea*)	5–9	Dense clusters of orange-red berries appear in late summer and persist into winter. In smaller gardens, train this shrub as an espalier, or opt for a dwarf version like 'Red Cushion' or 'Rudgers'.
sweet box (*Sarcococca ruscifolia*)	6–9	In winter, fragrant white flowers provide soft contrast to the dark green leaves. After flowers are done blooming, small, glossy red and blue berries add interest.
Texas mountain laurel (*Sophora secundiflora*)	7–10	Small stature, evergreen foliage, and deeply fragrant purple blooms that appear in late winter make this small tree a standout.
coral bark Japanese maple (*Acer palmatum*)	5–9	Coral bark maple is most spectacular when out of leaf. Branches intensify to a richly colored coral-red in winter, resulting in a striking cold-season focal point.

clockwise, from top left
Darwin's barberry, saucer magnolia, sweet box, coral bark Japanese maple, Texas mountain laurel, scarlet firethorn

right Seasonal touches like pinecones and holly give this winter container a festive flair.

far right Tropical foliage anchors a summer-themed container.

opposite A grouping of fall containers is accented with colorful pumpkins.

Seasonal containers

To inject a small or temporary note of the seasons into the garden, consider treating seasonality as an accessory by taking advantage of containers.

Noted Oklahoma garden designer Helen Weis specializes in creating original container plantings packed with colorful lushness. Her containers span the seasons, creating an ever-changing gallery of landscape focal points. One of her strategies is to think beyond traditional plants. In winter, that might mean incorporating natural branches, sugar pine cones or fresh, local evergreens. Spring's focus on bulbs and flowers in soft pastels echoes the emerging pink, white, and creamy yellow blooms of the surrounding landscape. Ornamental cabbage and kale may find their way into her fall designs. As summer is the longest season in her part of the country, she focuses on color and composition and often builds a container around tropical plants with bold foliage, like cannas or banana trees. As Helen says, "It's all about incorporating the things that move you or that you admire about the season, whichever season you may be in."

While foliage plants in a mix of colors and textures should make up the backbone of your plant choices, your garden is also the perfect place to celebrate the changes that nature brings throughout the year. Whether you opt for containers or one or two carefully chosen plants to usher in each season, don't let limited space stop you from designing a backyard with year-round appeal.

a sense of place, regardless of space

What makes a house a home? A house provides shelter, but it is the people and pets who dwell there, the collections it holds, and the memories made within that help turn it into a home. Spaces that reflect our personal style and interests are the ones we treasure.

A home isn't defined by four walls alone. Your landscape also has the potential to be more than a sum of its parts — it can create a welcoming first impression, host memorable family meals and events, and act as a calming refuge from the stresses of everyday life. Landscapes have a real power to evoke emotional responses in us — yes, even suburban backyards. Devoting as much attention to how your outdoor space affects you as you do to your indoor space will dramatically increase your enjoyment of your entire home.

Vivid shades highlight Keeyla Meadows' eclectic garden.

This Nebraska garden is filled with native species to attract native pollinators and wildlife.

Although the process of creating a garden uniquely your own begins by addressing lifestyle needs—both now and for the future—it doesn't stop with that. Aesthetics, atmosphere, and personal connection are also part of the mix. One way to tie all these aspects together is to design your garden with a sense of place in mind.

What exactly is a sense of place? It can be defined in different ways. *Geography Dictionary* interprets it as "either the intrinsic character of a place or the meaning people give to it, but, more often, a mixture of both." This definition is useful because it breaks the concept into two distinct but complementary ideas. Looking at each will help you create a truly meaningful yard of your own. While all gardens benefit from embracing this concept, smaller backyards are uniquely suited to embody this approach, as less real estate means that a few simple changes may be all that's required to evoke a sense of place.

A rustic chair accents
a garden.

The Regional Connection

Intrinsic character is what should connect your garden to the natural world
around you. For many years, American backyards had a tendency to look a lot alike:
plenty of lawn, a few ornamental trees, and a reliable collection of roses or other
flowering shrubs. As author, educator, and landscape architect Chris Grampp dis-
cusses in his book *From Yard to Garden*, this standardized version has been with us
for close to 100 years; it began in the 1920s and 1930s when garden clubs and civic
beautification committees heavily promoted a landscape of shrubs and lawns for the
newly invented and growing garden suburbs. By the 1930s, nearly all of the garden
advice in books, newspapers and magazines advocated for lawn and foundation
shrubs. In fact, a 1937 *Better Homes and Gardens* article extolling the virtues of

Bold, tropical foliage marks this unmistakably as a Florida garden.

regional architecture features virtually identical lawn and foundation plantings in each yard — regardless of whether or not they do anything to enhance the character of the houses themselves.

No one could mistake a Florida beach for a Nebraska prairie, or a Maryland greensward for a Southwest desert. So why should our yards continue to look the same, when we live in vastly different regions with individual characteristics worth celebrating? A heightened appreciation for ecology and protecting the environment has resulted in a cultural shift away from a homogenous view of the ideal suburban backyard and toward private gardens that reflect their natural surroundings.

At first, incorporating regionally inspired elements into your backyard might seem like an overly ambitious idea or a concept too large to implement, but it's often easier than you think. In fact, allowing the region to drive your decisions has practical and financial as well as aesthetic implications. Most important, choosing plants that are native or culturally well adapted to your region means your garden will be much more likely to thrive. Plants suitable for your climate or zone are not only hardier, they generally need less maintenance and outside intervention in the form of supplemental water or chemicals and fertilizers. They also simply *look* like they belong in the landscape.

The first step is to familiarize yourself with plants that perform well where you live. Walking around the neighborhood to see what's been planted is not the most reliable way, as many mature gardens planted years ago don't necessarily reflect this newer movement that embraces native choices. Spending a little research time up front will mean less wasted time and energy down the road. Fortunately, most areas have lots of free and easily accessible resources to help you, such as:

- Cooperative extensions of public universities and/or Master Gardener services
- Public botanical gardens
- Community or government-sponsored demonstration gardens
- Local garden blogs

left Succulents are an ideal plant choice for areas of the country where they naturalize.

above Bluebonnets are regionally appropriate in many areas of the country.

regional resources across the country

Wherever you live, there are almost certainly resources for learning plants that are native to or well adapted to the local region. These sources can be invaluable in helping you select plants that will naturally thrive in your garden, with a minimum of time and effort. Examples of these regional programs include the Lady Bird Johnson Wildflower Center at the University of Texas at Austin; the Plant Select program in conjunction with the Denver Botanic Gardens and Colorado State University; Gold Medal Plants through the Pennsylvania Horticultural Society; Arboretum All-Stars tested and recommended by the University of California at Davis Arboretum; and Great Plant Picks, offered by the Elisabeth C. Miller Botanical Garden in Seattle to gardeners west of the Cascade Mountains. If you're not sure of a program in your area, a little research into the resources listed previously should result in a list of recommended plants.

Creating a sense of place by tapping into the intrinsic character of your region can go beyond plants. Choosing hardscape options that are locally quarried—such as Pennsylvania bluestone, Michigan fieldstone, or salt and pepper granite in Washington state—not only connects your garden with your community, but can also save you money as local materials are often less expensive. The same is true for garden ornaments. Why choose the same garden gnome as your cousin living several states away, when you can find something local at a craft fair?

Giving a Space Personal Meaning

The character and individuality we give to a garden is also an important way of imbuing it with a strong sense of place. We are hardwired to attach meaning to places we think of as home, and to value those places above others. That's why the more our own yards and landscapes—regardless of their size—reflect our backgrounds, beliefs, and sense of personal style, the stronger the sense of place, and the greater our enjoyment of them.

How exactly is home defined? Memory can play a powerful role. According to census data, almost 40 percent of the population does not consider the "place in your heart you consider to be home" to be the place where they currently live. Not surprisingly, this strong connection to memories of our upbringing encourages a tendency to try and recreate the landscapes of childhood. While understandable—given that we are a nation of transplants often living in significantly smaller spaces and in entirely different climate zones than the ones in which we grew up—this approach rarely leads to a low-maintenance, high-impact backyard.

While honoring connections to our past might seem like a satisfying and intuitive idea, choosing ecologically inappropriate plants that will require excessive water, fertilizers, or other forms of intervention to survive—if they even do—will not make for a successful or enjoyable garden in the long run. Still, anyone who has tried to stick with a diet knows how impossible it is to deprive yourself of your favorite things indefinitely. Better to enjoy a modest taste of high-quality chocolate every day than break down and gorge yourself on grocery-store sweets. This philosophy works for garden design as well. Instead of filling your garden with high-maintenance plants from half a country – or even half a world – away, include them in small, exquisitely thought-out doses in ways that are easily managed.

One option is to create a small space in the garden that is evocative of the landscape of your childhood. This could mean planting a scaled-down version of a woodland garden if you miss the shady, natural spaces of your childhood home, or incorporating rocks and boulders if you grew up amid the granite slopes of New England. Alternatively, your nod to the past might be as simple as taking one feature that resonates strongly with you, such as one particular plant or a garden structure, and finding a home for it in your new landscape.

The challenge with choosing one or two special plants is integrating them successfully into the cultural conditions of the rest of the backyard. This is where containers come in. A container garden is already an artificial environment, so providing supplemental nutrients or water that the rest of your garden has no need for can be done on a small, manageable scale. Containers also lend themselves to overwintering indoors – much easier than attempting to protect a sensitive plant in the ground. Cold- and wet-weather dwellers who miss the low-water, heat-loving succulents from the Southwest can satisfy their cravings with pots that can be relocated inside when cold weather and rains begin.

Succulents can help conjure a sense of the arid Southwest.

Of course, sometimes the desire to recreate home is too strong to be satisfied with a container or two. I frequently run into this when working with transplants from the Midwest or Northeast, who wistfully hand me lists filled with plants that I know won't thrive in their new California home. Long before I became a designer, however, I saw firsthand how powerfully motivating the drive to recreate a familiar environment can be. The first thing my mother has done at every house she's lived in since she moved away from the East Coast is to plant a crazy number of trees – all in an effort to reproduce the dappled green light of the leafy, wooded landscape she left behind. No amount of tree planting will transform a sun-drenched, water-parched California vista into the humid, humusy landscape of North Carolina, however, and over the years she's reached a compromise – a small area for the old-fashioned, water-loving annuals, balanced by a commitment to more culturally appropriate plants.

If my mother's story strikes a chord with you, there are other ways to bridge the gap. Sometimes it isn't necessary to recreate a plant memory exactly. Simply look for plants that share the characteristics of your long-time favorites, and your garden can continue to be a haven for treasured memories. The trick is to figure out what it is about a certain plant that makes it special, then choose something zone-appropriate for your new home that offers the same experience. Miss the powerful fragrance of frost-tender angel's trumpet (*Brugmansia* spp.)? Cold-weather gardeners can substitute virgin's bower (*Clematis virginiana*). Pining for the richly colored lilacs of your East Coast youth? Try California lilac (*Ceanothus* spp.) or Texas ranger bush

(*Leucophyllum frutescens*). If you're not sure where to start, try asking at your local nursery or at a public university's extension service.

Signature style

Gardens don't just express where we come from — they are an opportunity to reflect who we are today. Much of this book is focused on incorporating lifestyle elements into your garden, but in addition to being a space created with the outdoor activities you love in mind, your backyard can also be a reflection of you. The best landscapes are more than just a sum of their parts; they are spaces that reflect the uniqueness of their creators and owners. This is another area where small gardens truly shine. Like the examples profiled here, the limited canvas of a modest backyard means the personal touches you add will naturally take center stage.

A few years ago, I attended an open garden tour in Berkeley sponsored by the Garden Conservancy. On the tour, I visited two gardens within a few miles of each other, similar in size, but completely different in every other way. The first stop on the tour was the personal garden of noted sculptor and designer Keeyla Meadows. Bursting with flowers, vines, sculptures, and whimsy, this is one of the most uniquely colorful gardens I've ever had the pleasure of visiting. In her backyard, Keeyla takes every rule or suggestion on color combining and promptly reinvents them to suit herself. The garden is not limited to one color palette, so sections move from analogous groupings of sizzling shades of red, orange, and yellow, to cool-toned combos dominated by neon greens and soft purples, to areas where pretty much every swatch on the color wheel has seemingly joined the party. Rejecting the idea of negative space, or a quiet place to rest the eye, containers, walls, benches, and doors — and a riot of plant life — are all equally alive with color. Keeyla's artistic hand is particularly evident in her whimsically crafted containers, which contain equally dynamic plant combinations.

The next stop on the tour that day was the oft-photographed garden of artist and sculptor Marcia Donahue. Although equally lush and filled with artistic touches, Marcia's garden in all other ways offers an entirely different experience. Eschewing the bright colors and flowers that make Keeyla's garden a visual tour de force, Marcia has opted for a monochromatic plant palette with towering bamboo and tropical foliage, something akin to a miniature jungle. Instead of taking center stage, the plants share the spotlight with an extensive sculpture gallery, with objects carefully sited so that foliage and artwork complement one another. Although at first the myriad statuary, found objects, and mosaics can seem random, themes quickly emerge. Oversized malas (a set of Hindu rosary beads generally numbering 108) that Marcia sculpts from ceramic are draped over branches or wrapped around tree trunks. Bowling balls become the quirky building blocks for sculptures and groupings scattered throughout the garden. Throughout, the concept of scale is turned on its head, with an eclectic mix of literal and whimsical statuary.

Evergreen California lilac (*Ceanothus* spp.) is an attractive alternative to lilacs (*Syringa* spp.) in West Coast gardens lacking the winter chill lilacs need to thrive.

top left The chartreuse and purple of a ceramic container sculpted by Keeyla Meadows echo the hues of a backdrop wall and surrounding plants.

bottom Bowling balls stacked in unusual ways are quirky elements in Marcia Donahue's garden.

top right Pink ceramic feet created by Marcia Donahue's daughter, Sara Tool, make a whimsical planter waiting to be discovered along a garden path.

above Fruit from trees in Theresa Loe's garden is used to make jam, which may later show up in one of her signature jamtinis.

right A bedspring once destined for the landfill is pressed into service in Theresa Loe's urban homestead garden.

While artists' gardens like these are beyond the scope of what most of us have the skill or desire to create, they do drive home the fact that our backyards can be more than just destinations. Located in high-density Los Angeles, Theresa Loe's tiny backyard is less than .10 acre, and makes the case that a garden doesn't need to be large to create the ultimate sense of place—in this instance, by reflecting the values and lifestyle of the family that lives there. Creator of the popular website and podcast *Living Homegrown*, Theresa has transformed her suburban backyard into a miniature urban homestead, where her lively flock of chickens scratch contentedly against the backdrop of a sumptuous garden bursting with seasonal produce. Rather than confining edibles to a few raised beds banished to the sidelines, vegetables, herbs, and dwarf fruit trees are mixed throughout the landscape. Theresa captures the seasonal flavors of her garden in pickles, ferments, and other preserves and has even been known to incorporate her homemade jam into the occasional jamtini (a cocktail made with jam). Beyond feeding her family of four, the backyard is a gathering place that Theresa and her husband Rick view as an opportunity to share their values of responsible living and sustainable practices with their two sons. Found objects rescued from the landfill are used creatively throughout the landscape to train vines, prop up cucumbers, or simply provide a touch of whimsy. A favorite family weekend activity is biking around the neighborhood visiting garage sales, in hopes of discovering an unwanted castoff that can be repurposed into a family treasure.

Despite the short growing season in blustery Chicago, wellness lifestyle advocate Shawna Coronado spends as much time as possible in her garden, which features an eclectic mix of edibles, flowers, and DIY projects. When she inherited her grandmother's treasured collection of glass balls and insulators, she knew she wanted to display this happy reminder in a space that has personal meaning for her. Rather than store them away, she put them to use as a fanciful border in her garden.

Just as a home often includes family photos and cherished heirlooms, think of your garden as an extension of your living space, and be brave enough to make it equally personalized — it can serve as a place to acknowledge and honor our family connections as well as to express our own personalities. Whether it is to share your sense of family, reinforce your values, or display your own creativity, incorporating artwork or collections that you love is an easy, affordable, and rewarding way to stake out your ownership of a space. However you choose to personalize your less is more garden, letting go of a traditional, conforming view of what a backyard should be can be an empowering and satisfying experience. To paraphrase Dorothy in *The Wizard of Oz*, if there really *is* no place like home, why not make yours uniquely your own?

left A ceramic dress sculpture by artist Keeyla Meadows adds garden whimsy and memorable personal style.

above Special memories can enhance time in the garden. Shawna Coronado incorporated her grandmother's set of glass insulators as a colorful border.

Metric Conversions

Inches	Centimeters	Feet	Meters
¼	0.6	1	0.3
⅓	0.8	2	0.6
½	1.3	3	0.9
¾	1.9	4	1.2
1	2.5	5	1.5
2	5.1	6	1.8
3	7.6	7	2.1
4	10	8	2.4
5	13	9	2.7
6	15	10	3
7	18		
8	20		
9	23		
10	25		

Temperatures

degrees Celsius = 0.55 × (degrees Fahrenheit - 32)

degrees Fahrenheit = (1.8 × degrees Celsius) + 32

To convert length:	Multiply by:
Yards to meters	0.9
Inches to centimeters	2.54
Inches to millimeters	25.4
Feet to centimeters	30.5

Additional Reading and Resources

Recommended Reading

Brenzel, Kathleen Norris et al., eds. 2015. *Sunset Western Garden Book of Easy-Care Plantings: The Ultimate Guide to Low-Water Beds, Borders, and Containers*. New York: Oxmoor House.

DiSabato-Aust, Tracy. 2007. *50 High-Impact, Low-Care Garden Plants: Tough-but-Beautiful Plants Anyone Can Grow*. Portland, OR: Timber Press.

Easton, Valerie. 2009. *The New Low-Maintenance Garden*. Portland, OR: Timber Press.

Eierman, Colby. 2012. *Fruit Trees in Small Spaces: Abundant Harvests from Your Own Backyard*. Portland, OR: Timber Press.

Frey, Kate, and Gretchen LeBuhn. 2016. *The Bee-Friendly Garden: Design an Abundant, Flower-Filled Yard that Nurtures Bees and Supports Biodiversity*. Berkeley, CA: Ten Speed Press.

Hadden, Evelyn. 2012. *Beautiful, No-Mow Yards*. Portland, OR: Timber Press.

Kingsbury, Noel. 2016. *The New Small Garden: Contemporary Principles, Planting and Practice*. London: Francis Lincoln.

Morris, Jennifer Renjilian et al., eds. 2013. *Fine Gardening Pocket Gardens: Design Ideas for Small Space Gardening*. Newtown, CT: Taunton Press.

Penick, Pam. 2013. *Lawn Gone! Low-Maintenance, Sustainable, Attractive Alternatives for Your Yard*. Berkeley, CA: Ten Speed Press.

Slatalla, Michelle. 2016. *Gardenista: The Definitive Guide to Stylish Outdoor Spaces*. New York: Artisan.

Wingate, Marty. 2012. *Landscaping for Privacy: Innovative Ways to Turn Your Outdoor Space into a Peaceful Retreat*. Portland, OR: Timber Press.

Online Nurseries

Annie's Annuals and Perennials
www.anniesannuals.com

High Country Gardens
www.highcountrygardens.com

Plant Delights Nursery
www.plantdelights.com

Acknowledgments

Isaac Asimov wrote "Writing is a lonely job," and while anyone who has spent the better part of a year alone in front of a computer screen, struggling to commit their ideas to paper, can appreciate this point of view, I could never have written this book without the generous support and assistance of family, friends, and colleagues.

Sourcing photographs that reflect the diverse beauty of small gardens all across the country was one of the most challenging aspects of bringing this book to life. Thank you to all the designers and photographers who so generously shared their photos with me: Linda Lehmusvirta, Benjamin Vogt, John Beaudry, Pam Penick, Anna Brooks, Katie Weber, Kelly Kilpatrick, Killian O'Sullivan, Michelle Derviss, Tina Henricksen, Jenny Peterson, Katie Elzer-Peters, and Wickie Rowland. A special thanks to Hunter Ten Broeck and Rebecca Sweet for coming to my rescue over and over again with just the right images, and to my clients Gale Gettinger and Tai Williams for their willingness to photograph local gardens.

Thank you to Janet Sluis for providing photos from the Sunset Western Garden Collection and the Southern Living Collection and to professional photographers Jude Parkinson-Morgan, Doreen Wynja, and Kerry Michaels for tirelessly combing through their portfolios in search of the perfect images for me.

Thank you to the gardeners and designers who allowed me to share their design ideas and inspiring personal spaces: Shawna Coronado, Marcia Donahue, Theresa Loe, Carla and Lennart Lundstrom, Keeyla Meadows, Janet Miller, and Helen Weis.

Thank you to my editors at Timber Press, Juree Sondker, who started this journey with me; Stacee Lawrence, whose deft editing skills helped me find my best voice; and Julie Talbot, who left no stone unturned to make this the best book it could possibly be. Thank you also to my agent, Andrea Barzvi, for her thoughtful advice and ongoing support.

A few individuals deserve special thanks for their particularly impactful contributions: Catharine Cooke and Patricia St. John, for allowing me to showcase their beautiful designs; Lynn Felici-Gallant, for providing both encouragement and lush photography; Scott Hokunson, for his construction expertise; and Saxon Holt, not only for his lovely photos of the Lundstrom garden, but also for his thoughtful advice on choosing the best ones to feature in the book. Thank you also to Steve Aitken for his generosity in writing such a perfect foreword.

And finally, thank you to my husband Nicholas Bowerman for tirelessly reading draft after draft, and politely pretending not to notice all the times I was still in my bathrobe when he returned home from work.

Photography, Design, and Location Credits

Photos are by the author unless otherwise credited.

Adobe Stock

shaiith, pages 12–13

John R. Beaudry, pages 118 bottom, 205 left, design by John R. Beaudry for the Stern garden.

Joan S. Bolton, page 23, design by Joan S. Bolton of Santa Barbara Garden Design for the Joan T. Seaver Kurze garden.

Anna Brooks, page 96, above right

Catharine Cooke, page 17, design by Catharine Cooke and Ian Gribble

Shawna Coronado at shawnacoronado.com, page 211 above

Courtesy of Annie's Annuals and Perennials, pages 98 top, 79 bottom right, 160 right, 193 bottom right

Courtesy of the Southern Living Plant Collection, page 185 top right

Courtesy of the Sunset Western Garden Collection, pages 143 bottom left, 183 center left, 183 bottom left

Michelle Derviss, page 38, design by Michelle Derviss

Katie Elzer-Peters, page 125 bottom left

C. L. Fornari, page 146

Gale Gettinger, pages 8, 26, 133, 134–135, the garden of Gale Gettinger and Richard Ash; 143 top right, 144, 169 below right; 34–35, 149, 165, 172–173, 114 right, 129 top right, the garden of Janet and Dan Miller

Tina Henricksen, page 95 bottom left

Saxon Holt, pages 6–7, 62 above, center right, and bottom, 63, 64, 65 bottom left, bottom right, and top, 66, 67 top, center, and bottom, 95 bottom right, 110 bottom, 125 center left; 195 center right, design by Susan Morrison for the Lundstrom garden

Saxon Holt for the Sunset Western Garden Collection, pages 95 top center, 183 top left, 193 center right

istock

Terryfic3D, page 161

cubanman, page 137 left

Johnny Greig, page 14 left

JDwow, page 109 bottom left

msterlin, page 109 top right,

aimintang, page 109 center left

richjem, page 136

DavidByronKeener, page 147

Lynn Felici-Gallant, pages 191 top right; 56 top and bottom, 57 top, design by Catharine Cooke and Ian Gribble for the Kolod garden

Kelly Kilpatrick, page 205 right

Linda Lehmusvirta, pages 31 top, 145 left

Theresa Loe, pages 210 right and left, garden of Theresa Loe

Kerry Michaels, pages 27 top, 191 center left, 157, 203

Keeyla Meadows, pages 200–201, 211, design and garden of Keeyla Meadows

Millette, pages 57 center, 79 center second left, bottom left, and center far right, page 96 left, 97 bottom, 99 left, 125 center right, 143 bottom right, 191 bottom left, 197 bottom left, 185 bottom left, 193 center left, 57 center left

Killian O'Sullivan, pages 44, 59, garden design by Kelly Kilpatrick, architectural design by Killian O'Sullivan AIA, for Lynne Deegan-McGraw

Jude Parkinson-Morgan, pages 107 bottom; 139; 188 top right; 20, design by Huettl & IRI for the Sanchez garden; 29, 100–101, 112, 126, design by Patricia St. John APLD of St. John Landscapes for the Tyhurst and Hayes garden; 32, 131, design by Katrine Thomas, Fine Gardener for the Doerr Toppin garden; 80, 111 left, 176, design by Jeannie Fitch of Garden Nest for the Jones garden; 81, 107 top left, design by Linda Middleton APLD of Terralinda Design; 85, design by Nina Mullen of Mullen Designs for the Tanovic garden; 88, design by Jeannie Fitch of Garden Nest; 79 top, 106 left, design and garden of Ann Nichols; 118 top, design by Roxy Wolosenko of Roxy Designs; 154–155, design by Roxy Wolosenko of Roxy Designs for the Rose-Lerman garden; 168, design by Patricia St. John APLD of St. John Landscapes for the Chaves garden

Pam Penick, pages 98 bottom, 195 top left

Jenny Peterson, page 193 top left

Wickie Rowland, page 99 right

John Shewey, page 106 bottom

Shutterstock

vallefrias, page 93 bottom right

Patricia St John APLD, pages 83; 69 top and bottom, 70, 71 top, center, bottom, design by Patricia St. John APLD of St. John Landscapes for the WaiChee Khoong garden

Amy Stewart, page 152, design by Susan Morrison

Rebecca Sweet, pages 18, 137, design by Rebecca Sweet; 25 top left, 140, 197 left center, 197 right center

Hunter Ten Broeck, pages 47, design by Hunter Ten Broeck; 109 right center; 114 left; 116–117, design by Judith Phillips for the Marilyn Underwood garden; 122–123, design by Hunter Ten Broeck; 195 left center

Benjamin Vogt, pages 189; 202, design by Monarch Gardens LLC; 145 right

Katie Weber, pages 91, 93 center right, design and garden of Katie Weber of Katie Weber Landscape Design

Helen Weis pages 198 left, design by Helen Weis for the garden of Dr. and Mrs. Tkach; 199, design by Helen Weis for the Cole Richardson garden; 198 right, design by Helen Weis for the garden of Ray and Sherri Carter

Wikimedia Commons

Used under a Creative Commons Attribution-Share Alike 3.0 Unported license:

Michal Wolf, page 160 left

EnLorax, page 125 bottom right

Dominicus Johannes Bergsma, page 109 bottom right

Carl Dennis, Auburn University, Bugwood.org, page 25 bottom right

Used under a Creative Commons Attribution-Share Alike 2.0 Generic license:

bastus917, page 191 center right

liz west, page 158

Tai Williams, pages 43, 132, design by Susan Morrison for the James garden; pages 14, 28, 31 bottom, 42, 141, 74–75, design by Susan Morrison for the Williams garden; 50 opposite top and bottom, 51 above and above left, design by Susan Morrison for the Morrison-Bowerman garden

Doreen Wynja, Eye of the Lady, pages 2, 151, design and garden of Linda Ernst of Dancing Ladies Garden, sculpture by Cynthia Spencer; 27 below; 46; 87, design by Lori Scott; 16, 104, 177, design and garden of Marina Wynton, Olivine Land LLC; 41, design by Leonard Foltz and Fred Weisensee, Dancing Oaks Nursery; 103, design and garden of Linda Hannan of Hannan Garden Design; 138; 164, design by Janice Palma-Glennie for the Keuhlewind garden; 166, design and garden of Bruce Hegna of Nature/Nurture Landscape Design; 174, design by Barbara Hilty Landscape Design for Marilyn Mauch garden; 195 top right

Doreen Wynja for Monrovia, pages 93 bottom left, 185 top center, 186 left

Additional Design and Homeowner Credits

Garden of Janet and Dan Miller, pages 76, 162–163

Design by Susan Morrison for the Corbin garden, pages 82, 180

Garden of Kate Mendenhall, pages 90, 129 left

Design by BJ Ledgerwood for the Giffen garden, page 128 top left and bottom right

Garden of Linda LaRue Brown, pages 178–179

Design and garden of Keeyla Meadows, pages 156, 200–201, 207, 209 top left, 211 left

Design and garden of Marcia Donahue, pages 208 bottom and top right

Design and garden of Ann Nichols, page 37

Index

Nicholas Bowerman

California landscape designer **Susan Morrison** is a nationally recognized authority on small-space garden design. She writes articles on the topic, presents her talks on the subject to garden enthusiasts all over the country, and has shared small-garden strategies on the ground-breaking PBS series, *Growing a Greener World*. Susan's designs have been featured in publications including the *San Francisco Chronicle*, *Cottages and Bungalows*, and *Fine Gardening*, where she also contributes articles on design and plant selection. She has also served as editor in chief of *The Designer*, a digital magazine produced by the Association of Professional Landscape Designers. Susan maintains active volunteer status as a Master Gardener, and serves on the ReScape California Advisory Committee.

Most important, Susan knows firsthand the challenges and rewards of gardening in a small space. Her own 30-by-60-foot backyard is a laboratory for fresh design ideas, a test garden for new plants, and the most popular room of her home on a summer evening. For more, visit Susan's website at http://celandscapedesign.com.